...AND THIS IS HOW IT ENDS

*The True Story of Minivans, Switchblade Combs,
and the Homeless*

Jen Sky

Cover Art/Design: Lee Adam Herold and Jennifer Neil

Audio: Nick Sciarappa

Scripture quotations have been taken from the *New American Bible, Revised Edition (NABRE)* copyright © 2011 unless otherwise specified.

Photos printed with permission from Christy Pendarvis

Copyright © 2018 Jen Sky

ISBN-13: 978-1720902164

ISBN-10: 172090216X

To my grandmas, who taught me that a meal is more than just a meal. I miss you.

CONTENTS

THE COVER

The photo on the cover was taken by me at one of our homeless Welcome Wagons. The "blessing" was for a woman suffering with brain cancer. She had finally come indoors, but her apartment was dirty and completely empty. Her cupboards were bare. After giving her the cross in the picture, she prominently displayed it in the entrance to the apartment. As I was leaving I quickly snapped this picture of the cross, not realizing the cigarette butt was right next to it. As I reflect on our work with the homeless, it seems fitting that there would be a cross next to a cigarette.

As Oscar Wilde said, "Every saint has a past, and every sinner has a future." That's what this picture and this entire book says to me.

…AND THIS IS HOW IT ENDS.

FOREWARD

Sharon Boone, Co-Founder Outreached Arms Homeless Organization
Pittsburgh, Pennsylvania

Ordinary people doing extraordinary deeds.

This was the phrase used when I was honored as a Hometown Hero for my work as a co-founder of Outreached Arms, a nonprofit that serves the homeless. I believe this statement can also be used to describe the people in this book.

Uncomfortable. Isn't that how most people would describe their experience as they approach a homeless person holding a cardboard sign that reads, "Hungry. Please help?"

We ask ourselves, "Will they buy drugs or alcohol?"

"Why don't they just get a job?"

We don't allow ourselves to make eye contact.

Why? What are we afraid of?

Jen and I both found ourselves stepping out of our quaint communities, our flourishing churches, and our comfortable lives... for the uncomfortable. Like me, she began this journey with no idea where it would take her or how it would forever change her life.

As you begin reading this book, you will see how one woman and a few friends began a movement that started by bringing lunch for a few homeless. It has grown into an organization, Mission from Mars, that not only feeds approximately 150 people each Sunday afternoon, but ministers to homeless camps, helps find affordable housing, and has provided clothing, blankets, and tents for those in extreme need. You will see the incredible generosity of a community of neighbors, sports teams, scouts, and churches that have come together to give back.

As you turn the pages, you will learn what it is to be a homeless person. Jen paints a brutally honest picture of the unimaginable conditions the homeless live each day.

You may find yourself asking, "Why would anyone want to subject themselves, or their children, to come in contact with, talk with, or even hug these men and women who are so often thought of as undesirables?" For Jen, I think she asked herself the same questions. Her stories will tug on your heart and will have you laughing, crying, and asking the question, "What were they thinking?"

In this moving and inspiring portrayal, it is my hope that you will see homelessness differently - through the eyes of God. You will come to understand that the homeless are people much like you and me, who, for whatever reasons, have fallen on hard times. You will experience how serving the less fortunate causes change, not only in the lives of the homeless, but also in the volunteers who will be forever transformed.

When you give of yourself to help others, you cannot help but to be more kind, compassionate, giving, and caring - not only in serving, but in your day-to-day life. Maybe the next time you come across a homeless person, you will be able to look them in the eyes and see them for who they truly are – a child of God.

Sharon Boone
Co-Founder, Outreached Arms
First Presbyterian Church Pittsburgh
May, 2018

Chapter 1

THE UNLOVABLE

"To love means loving the unlovable. To forgive means pardoning the unpardonable. Faith means believing the unbelievable. Hope means hoping when everything seems hopeless."

G. K. Chesterton

How do you love the unlovable?

If you help a convicted child molester, or murderer, or drug dealer, what does that make you?

Would you give a serial killer a drink? A meal? A conversation?

What if they've converted? Changed?

What if they haven't?

These are the questions anyone who helps people in marginal situations has to wrestle with. What if the sleeping bag I gave out to a homeless man went to the arsonist on the news or a rapist?

What if the food you gave kept him alive?

What if you unwittingly helped a fugitive flee the law by giving him supplies?

How would you feel if you found out that a person you had helped was a convicted felon? I can tell you from personal experience how it feels - terrible!

"How many victims' lives does he have to destroy before the courts decide that he is a threat? Weren't the two eight year old girls enough?"

"This is shameful. How do you people sleep at night?"

"Do you have a conscience?"

These words could have been intended for me, or any of us who ministered to the homeless. Instead, they were posted by viewers on a local television website directed at the court system for releasing a sexual predator into our midst - a predator that had now disappeared and failed to report to his case officer.

We met the man in question while serving a lunch for the homeless on Pittsburgh's North Side. He had shown up like so many others, hungry, disheveled, and cold. Pittsburgh's winters are known for their freezing, damp temperatures, and this one was no different. The man was anxious to receive food, but kept his distance from the crowd of people. When he came into the food line we treated him like everyone else, doling out a generous helping of food and compassion.

We helped a man who had nothing and was living on the streets, giving him a tarp, some clothing, and a meal. Three days later, we saw his face on the local television news.

"Pittsburgh police looking for convicted sex offender"
April 28, 2016 WPXI news

Wpxi.com

Police issued this statement, *"Basically, he's on the run right now, so our major concern is especially (with him) being a sexually violent*

predator, that's a huge concern for us. We don't know his whereabouts,"
said Pittsburgh Police Detective Mike Veith, who is in charge of keeping
tabs on the city's 500-plus registered sex offenders.

Police were searching for a man who was convicted of crimes
against children, who had failed to register as a sex offender. The
man was a sexually violent predator, known for changing his
appearance drastically.

According to police, he had been on the run before. In his most
recent case, he had fondled and exposed himself to two eight year
old girls, the news report said.

Seeing the report on television and then reading the report online
was like being punched in the stomach. Just three days before, this
convicted sex offender had been at our lunch for the homeless. He
looked almost identical to his last mugshot picture. It wasn't the
first time we had seen him either - he had been a regular to our
Sunday meal.

Should I feel guilt that we provided food and some comfort to this
man police were pursuing? The people we were helping on the
streets were experiencing something more difficult than I could
have ever imagined possible. They were broken in a way I had
never seen - broken in their material poverty, broken in their
relationships with others, and for some, broken in their relationship
with God.

I didn't set out to write a story about the homeless, nor did I set
out to write a book. In fact, I had never once met a homeless
person before embarking on this incredible adventure. I may have
contributed to a cup on the side of the road, but mostly I walked
past, making myself look oblivious to those on the street. I had a
lot of preconceived notions about homelessness. Why don't they
get jobs? Are they on drugs? Are they mentally unstable?

While I fully expected to encounter people who were battling drug addiction, mental illness, and workplace instability, I didn't realize that most of the people I would meet on the street would be as human as the next person. Some were college educated, others were veterans, and many had spouses and children.

This book is about my journey, the stories I have heard, and how they have changed my perceptions of what it means to be homeless. It's also about the really tough questions.

Should we allow homeless people to live in encampment "camp" areas under bridges or at other locations?

Should we help those in need, no matter their past or criminal history?

More importantly, it's about seeing the story from a bigger picture. How did one small group of disconnected people come together to do great things and how can these acts of kindness spread all over our country and our world?

The question that I am asked the most is: "How in the world did you get to a place where you would end up telling homeless people's stories?" Before getting to that answer, I want to tell you a little bit about myself and my own personal story.

I had never really thought of myself as an outwardly religious person. I have always had faith and my belief in God, but was never really comfortable sharing that faith with others, or really talking about it. When asked by my parish priest why I go to church, I truthfully answered "because my husband drags me there." I was half joking, but couldn't really come up with a better answer.

While I have always felt a peace at church, I found mass difficult to fit into our busy lives. My husband and I have four young children, and most days are a whirlwind of activity. By the time

Sunday came around, I was often exhausted. Rather than longing for church, I wished for more time under the covers in bed.

I have taught a once-monthly Faith Formation class for the last few years. For those old style Catholics, we used to refer to this as CCD, although this version is an abbreviated one - you meet once monthly for two hours. My first exposure to homelessness was during my first year teaching. I wanted to touch on lessons of service and to share some information about soup kitchens with them. Having never myself been to a soup kitchen, I googled one and played the video to my students. Looking back, I laugh at myself for trying to teach a lesson about the homeless without any actual knowledge. The video I showed the class was from a soup kitchen in New York, not even in our local area.

About a year later, a friend of mine who was on the Board of Light of Life Rescue Mission, a local Christian mission, invited my husband and me to an event to raise money for the homeless of Pittsburgh. Friends of ours were planning to attend, and we decided to join the fun.

As we sat in the concourse at Heinz Field eating a delicious meal, drinking wine, and enjoying the company of friends, I couldn't help but feel my first twinge of *something* for the homeless. Our hosts showed videos of people whose lives had been changed by the Mission, but none of them truly resonated with me or struck a chord. They didn't make me cry or touch me deeply in my soul.

Homelessness was not my cause.

In my eyes, the homeless were still the scary, dirty looking people on the side of the road asking for money, but I was beginning to see more.

To support my friends' efforts at the shelter, I invited them to speak to my Faith Formation class. I offered to run a small drive for toiletry items like toothpaste, combs, soap, etc. that they would pass out at the Mission. While the kids were filling "blessing bags" for the homeless, something small happened that day that began to change how I thought about people living on the streets.

My friends, Kim and Rick, read a book by Monica Gunning to my class. The book, *A Shelter in Our Car*, chronicles the story of a girl of around eight years of age, coincidentally the age of my Faith Formation class. Following the death of her father, Zettie and her mother started living in their car. Zettie's mom cannot provide for them financially, and they are forced to do without - without food, without shelter, without warmth and security. The story touched me and the children in the classroom deeply, as we conjured images of young Zettie washing her face for school in the cold park fountain and sleeping in her car overnight.

There was something unbelievable about the story we were reading. Was it really possible that young girls could be living in cars in our area? Could there be homeless children nearby? More questions than answers began to percolate, but I didn't think much of it. I didn't drive to the city often, and didn't have much exposure to the homeless to ponder the questions very deeply.

Not long after Kim and Rick's visit to my class, I saw a post on Facebook from an acquaintance. She was the mother of my son's friend and not someone I knew well. This posting was another glimpse, as I look back, where I could see God guiding and directing me to the homeless without my awareness. In her Facebook post, Natalie, my "friend," posted of her desire to help the homeless. She was wondering if anyone else felt compelled. If so, they should private message her.

The fact that I saw this post still baffles me today - the chances being so small, especially considering it wasn't a popular post and Natalie wasn't even a close friend. But I did see her post, and I did respond.

I responded in a way that I am starting to find typical of myself. I saw a problem - "she wanted to do more for the homeless but didn't know how"- and I saw a simple solution, I would direct her to Light of Life Mission, the one Kim and Rick represented to my Faith Formation class. *Simple. Easy. Unattached.*

It didn't exactly go as planned. That first conversation through Facebook Messenger consumed my entire evening. When I mentioned my friends and Light of Life, Natalie told me about meeting homeless people on the street, cooking meals for them, ferreting out the imposter homeless (people who prey on sympathies and panhandle). My mind was truly spinning. I had never once given any real thought to people that were homeless.

I kept trying to direct the conversation back to helping with the Mission, serving a meal in the soup kitchen, or collecting blessing bags as our class did. As you will see from our conversation below, I said very little. This is the first, but not the last time, Natalie would begin to inspire me and others.

I look back at that early naiveté and it makes me smile. God has plans for us that aren't in our comfort zone, and this whole conversation took me out of mine. That conversation on January 11, 2016 began what could only be called a transformational journey.

The conversation went like this:

Natalie:

Jan. 11, 2016 9:36 PM

Hey Jen! There are several (actually many) groups doing sustainable work for the Pittsburgh homeless. When I spoke to a few homeless guys this weekend, I heard a different perspective and I want to meet an immediate need. There are a lot of donations that are being misused (men acting homeless and then selling the items on the street). So, I'm trying to sort that out in my conscience, but instead of not giving, I'm just doing something else.

I am starting with 2 things.

1) They are in need of meals during lunch. The Mission provides breakfast and dinner. I specifically wanted to create "John's Meal." John was a homeless guy I talked to for awhile and wanted to teach me the streets. He taught me so much. There are a lot of guys downtown out for a 'good' meal and a handout and they don't really need it. He said, "To find those guys and women who are going to die this winter, make this meal." It is beans and veggie soup, no spices or salt, bread and plain salad.

He said about 10 men and women will really want this meal - even though it's plain. Those are the ones who need ministered to.

So one area I will need help with is anyone who wants to make, donate and/or serve the meal. I didn't post this publicly because I didn't want to invite FB friends that I don't really know to my house to make the soup. So I'm keeping that part for peeps I know. I plan to have a veggie chopping party for those interested.

2) I have the names of several homeless people that need, or are interested in Jesus. I started writing in Bibles. Highlighting verses, writing encouraging notes, just personalizing it. Sometimes not anything related to the Bible - even "sometimes I'm nervous when someone begs me for money. I'm working on that. We all have things we are working on." The street minister is giving the 'used' Bibles out to specific people. The first three received theirs yesterday. They cried. Others around them said they wanted one.

You'll soon find out that I'm a little bit behind Natalie – typically we have found my learning curve to be about three weeks later. It's now a joke between us, but the conversation continued...

Jen: *Interesting - happy to help but how is this sustainable?*

Natalie: *This is not sustainable.*

*The Mission and the larger organizations need to create the sustainable models, but there is an immediate need - **people actually dying and can't get to the Mission**. I saw a woman that I don't think will make it this winter.*

Jen: *So your idea is a one day soup---and passing out Bibles? Or is there more? It is so sad.*

Natalie: *I'm putting together a longer email with more detailed thoughts, but it's two separate efforts.*

One is the meal - but not the meals they get from other groups that are 'tasty.' The plain beans and veggies will sort through the ones wanting handouts and the ones starving. The other is the Bibles. These go to specific people - the street minister knows them in camps and has a relationship with them. She has been giving me names and I pray for them. I started giving them the Bibles. I gave a homeless man a 'blessing bag.' It had deodorant and soap in it. He said "You can keep that for someone else. That won't keep me alive. I mostly want the socks and hand warmers."

At this point, I was overwhelmed by what Natalie was saying. What do you mean the homeless don't need the deodorant and soap we packed for them? It made me realize how little I knew about the homeless and what their needs really were. I had no idea what I was getting involved with, but I did remember the book Kim and Rick read about the little girl sleeping in her car.

I responded: *My friends from Light of Life brought a fantastic book to my class, "A Shelter in Our Car."*

Natalie: *I'll definitely check it out.*

Some of these guys won't go to the mission or even take donated clothes from the Xmas tree. (Gifts from local churches)

Jen: *We collected gloves - wish I would have thought of hand warmers.*

Natalie: *They said when another homeless man rummages through stuff and if they come from a camp with bed bugs, it spreads easily. So they wear the same old thing. Depressed me.*

Jen: *How did you get involved with this person?*

Natalie: *They hang in the park across from the Mission. Rob (my husband) and I went down with a street minister and gave out bags, socks, fruit, and talked with several. Other groups go down there to drop donated stuff.*

Jen: *Our friends said that there are 1500 homeless in Pgh, and only capacity at the missions to serve about 500-600. What made you go downtown?*

Natalie: *Yes - I'm sure they don't have the capacity or the volunteers. Some of these guys are also disabled.*

*Rob and I went to Miami over Christmas and there were many homeless where we went out to eat and shop. I didn't know what to do. **I wanted to talk but was scared. I wanted to help but didn't want them to buy drugs.** So I just prayed about* *it and then I encountered a woman in Mars, PA who was organizing a group donating for Mars Home for Youth. She also worked with the homeless. I talked to her and asked her if she actually knew them. She did and she does my direct deliveries. Rob is not ready to go into the camps yet for safety reasons.*

She proceeded to tell me that the street minister had mentioned that at one of the camps, there were needles and spoons lying around.

At this point in the conversation, I felt so lost. There was this whole world of need out there that I had no idea even existed, but I couldn't stop thinking about drugs. This was not my comfort zone! Conversations about a woman walking into homeless camps with needles and spoons lying around...not only am I not ready yet, NOT READY EVER!

My very pithy reply: *Scary. Let me know what you need help with and I will do my best.*

Natalie: *I'll keep you in the loop. It's small, but at least I know my money and time go directly to someone in need.*

I saw a guy take all the new stuff with tags and the homeless guy told me he will go sell it on the corner.

Just confused me. Homeless guy said they are called the parasites and feed off the good people trying to help.

So that was the end of a very long Facebook conversation with a person I barely knew talking about homeless people, drugs, ministering in homeless camps, and the like.

19

Seriously, what on earth am I getting myself into, I thought?

At that point, I decided to do nothing… to let the whole thing blow over. But God has a way of making sure you listen when he wants something from you, as I soon learned. And this was just the beginning.

Chapter 2

CHOPPING

"We rise by lifting others."

Robert Ingersoll

February 20, 2016 – Meal Making

Over a month had passed, and Natalie invited me to her home to cook the meal for John, the homeless man she had been talking with. We would be chopping, slicing, and dicing all from the safe confines of her suburban home. This I could do! Being Italian, I'm comfortable in the kitchen and I knew a friend of mine would be there, so I decided to go help.

I arrived on a Saturday at Natalie's home to find six or seven people I didn't know chopping away. We introduced ourselves, but mostly focused on our "work."

What should we chop?

What size pieces?

Sauté which vegetables?

What's going into this soup?

These questions floated in the air as we chopped, sautéed, and filled crock pots with veggies.

As we became engaged in our chopping tasks and a couple more people joined us, Natalie started to share stories - not in a way that I think she even realized she was doing. It was more of a response to our myriad of questions about how on earth she got involved in making a meal for the homeless.

It started with a discussion about John, her homeless "man on the street." He's the one she had been getting her information from, and she described him in vivid detail.

From his lucid moments, she described what he had been teaching her. He was keen to pass along lots of street smarts, including what the streets are like for a homeless person. He told her stories about people not having shoes, only layers of socks. This is February, where we were being pounded by snow, ice, and cold conditions. Our minds began to wander and think about what it would be like to be outdoors without shoes.

The questions flowed and Natalie continued. She told of Operation Safety Net and the Emergency Shelters and how they opened up when it was below 26 degrees outside. These are centers funded in large part by the government, whose aim is to ensure the homeless are cared for, particularly in the extreme cold conditions.

Natalie described her concern for people who were very literally close to death. She said that these shelters open when there is a true risk that the homeless will *freeze to death* on the street. I let it sink in that someone might actually freeze to death on the streets of my hometown. It was almost too sad to think about.

One of the people she described was a homeless woman named Yvonne. I didn't know her at the time, but Yvonne had been ill with pneumonia and was living on the freezing cold streets attempting to recover. We found out later that the street minister, Christy, had been giving her soup.

As I left Natalie's, I felt happy to have helped in a small way. We had prepared enough soup to feed about 100 people, and it was gratifying to know that someone who would have likely gone without would have some measure of comfort: a warm bowl of soup on a cold day. The food preparation was easy work. I enjoyed meeting the people at Natalie's and especially hearing her stories about the homeless. There was a sense of fellowship, of community, that bound us as we chopped together.

The following day, Natalie and her family, along with some of my fellow choppers, went downtown to serve. I was unable to go with them that day. Despite the feeling that I contributed something the day before by chopping, I also had an unsettled feeling. There were so many questions that needed answered: How did the meal service go? Had anyone been injured? Were they grateful? Was there enough food? Where would they eat their next meal? Would it be healthy? I had so many questions!

And then it hit me. That was it. The end. There would be no more lunches. No more feeding the homeless. I felt confused, almost in a state of disbelief. Natalie had just finished telling us how these people were literally close to death, how there was not one shelter serving a meal during the day on Sunday. She had told us about the street minister spoon feeding soup to the woman with pneumonia. One meal and then we were done, just like that.

While there had never been a plan for Natalie to continue with the lunches, I couldn't help but continue to question.

What will happen to these people, I asked myself?

What will happen to John?

Are people really going to starve?

Graduating from social media for our conversations, Natalie and I began talking on the phone. I peppered her with questions, and she tried to answer them for me.

"The street minister will continue doing as she had done before, scavenging for food leftovers from hotels or her own house. Random people will make a crock pot of food and will serve it when they can."

Everything would go on as it had been, in its own uncoordinated way. The way that it had been before I went to Natalie's house to chop vegetables.

"What about John? What about all of the people that showed up to eat? Who is going to feed them?" I asked Natalie.

At the time, I didn't know much about the homeless. As I have become more educated, I have learned that the Mission closes each day for those who were simply staying overnight. Those who were not registered in a shelter's residential program were asked to leave in the morning and could not return indoors until dinner. There are only so many that their programs can accommodate, leaving some people outdoors for the majority of the day.

What are they supposed to do all day on a Sunday?

In theory, I understood the concept. Send people out so they will work or not become too dependent. The missions do so much, from feeding to providing shelter, but they only have so much space. The reality was that it was freezing cold outside and there was nowhere for them to go. There are very few places available to the homeless to go inside to get warm, and it wasn't like they had spending money to check out the Science Center or any other point of interest.

Few restaurants are open on Sunday on the North Side of Pittsburgh, where the mission is located, and even fewer for lunch.

Even if there was a place for them to go inside to get warm, where would it be? How many places want a smelly, half-frozen homeless person walking in? It's not exactly good for business.

Most of the people who didn't work on Sunday were forced to sit in the park across the street from the Mission.

Where will they eat?

I wondered so much that it permeated my thoughts.

Many people had turned out for that first "John's Meal" and it underscored for me just how many homeless people there really were on the street. It was estimated that 100 people were served lunch that Sunday and we had made just enough food.

Monday was not a good day for me. Frustration settled in. It was hard to think that we had started this expectation of feeding the poor only to abandon them. I hadn't yet met these people, but I didn't want to abandon them. The idea that they were lacking a simple meal was tearing me up inside.

I kept thinking, what if the woman with pneumonia dies? What if John dies? I hadn't even met them, but I didn't want to let anyone down.

"I'll do it," I told Natalie.

"I'll cook the meal next weekend."

While she didn't exactly say "No," she was less than encouraging. Natalie didn't know me well, and she didn't think I could handle making a meal for 100 in just five days time. Not intimidated by the idea of cooking for a crowd, I accepted the challenge. Natalie made contingency plans for my failure (unbeknownst to me) and I sent a quick Facebook message to my friends:

Jen

February 22, 2016:

You may have seen some recent postings about a group of local moms and dads that created a group that is serving lunchtime meals to the homeless each Sunday, filling a need the local shelters can't. The group is also providing clothing, used Bibles, etc. in an attempt to meet urgent and immediate needs - sometimes very specific things for specific people, like a certain size pant for someone trying to get a job, or shovels for those trying to make money by shoveling snow. It will get cold again this week, so please think about and pray for the people living on the streets this week in our own neighborhood.

If you are interested in helping, please email, text, or private message me. I will be coordinating the meal making this Saturday at my house. As this is a big undertaking in a short amount of time (we will serve over 100 people), I would love to have some help in the cooking department (Sat at noon) and in the supplies department (we have a pretty big list of needs). There are some inspiring people coordinating this effort, particularly Natalie, and I am proud to support their good work.

The response was overwhelming. By the following day, I had assembled a team who were willing and eager to help.

Jen:

February 23, 2016

Hi Ladies,

I will be coordinating the homeless meal this weekend. Our job is to make a meal for 100 people. I really need help with the following:

meal prep on Saturday; people to donate supplies. Please let me know if you are interested and to what degree. Older kids who have good knife skills and are able to cook on the stovetop are permitted on Saturday. All kids and families (especially dads) are invited to serve on Sunday (lots of details below)!

Natalie had provided me with details about what they were trying to do in terms of food. I didn't realize it at the time, but Natalie had bought many supplies to help Christy in her homeless street ministry, including things like Sternos and chafing dishes to help keep the meal hot. The email she sent me, which I reposted, was the first set of "operating instructions" for this newly formed group - Mission from Mars.

Christy named Mission from Mars after a small city north of Pittsburgh. There was no formal group or organization, rather one woman and a friend who were visiting people in a park in the North Side. She had set up a Facebook page to share her encounters. I reposted some additional info from Natalie below:

Jen:

February 23, 2016 (continued)

Here are the details from Natalie (our fearless leader):
- Provide a meal for 100 people. We try to incorporate protein, starch and veggie. You can provide a very small dessert.
- We are not too controlling on the meal - whatever fits your budget and cooking skills.
- Mission from Mars will provide 5 Sternos/Chafing Dishes, tables, and trash can/bags.
- You provide food in alum trays to put into the Sternos, plates, utensils, serving utensils, napkins, drinks (bottled water) or water in

a cooler with cups.

- We had 55 people come yesterday and many wanted seconds, and we delivered to 16 in camps and 20 on the streets. Your team will not do encampment or street delivery. At the end of the meal, we will provide to-go containers that we will fill up with leftovers and those will go to the streets.

- LEADER: The organizer is pretty much the leader and just works to figure it out. Christy is on-site and when she is not, her friend Bonnie assists.

- LOCATION: It is across the street from the Mission in the park area.

- ARRIVAL: Set up is 11:30 to 12:00. Meal is served from 12:00 to 2. Cleanup after.

- HOW DO THEY KNOW? It's word of mouth and they just arrive. She's there every week with something and they line up.

When I read this now, I have to laugh. We sounded so put together, as if we had been doing this for years. In reality, the prior week was the first "big" meal, and even Christy had only started meeting and feeding the homeless in November, just a few months prior. I told my friends of my plans in this next post:

Jen:

I would like to get a group together for Saturday afternoon that will bring items needed to cook and serve, including the items above, such as aluminum trays, utensils, etc. We will prep the food that day, likely will take an hour or so if we have enough hands. There will be an opportunity for you to serve the meal on Sunday as well.

We will be making a heavy pasta dish with baked ziti, ricotta cheese, mozzarella cheese, peas and asparagus. We will make this dish casserole style. We could also consider adding a meat like meatballs or Italian sausage? One section would be made with sauce, the other with olive oil due to some with GERD. Whatever we make will need to be heated the next day, so we need to keep that in mind. We will prepare the food in large trays.

Leading up to Saturday, I will also collect items that could be distributed (clothing, shoes, coats, etc.)

If anyone wants to volunteer to shop, that would be awesome too! Natalie has some to-go containers for us to use. Just so that everyone knows, this is basically a pop-up group of people helping. It is not a registered charity, so no tax-deductions. Your gifts are going directly to people on the street who need it right now - and if you go on Sunday you can be one of the people fulfilling those needs.

Please let me know what you are thinking and if you would like to help this weekend. I will keep a list of who is coming on Saturday and what items have been donated.

One final note- we will collect donations (Men's) of coats, hats, gloves, scarves, shoes and boots (particularly anything with a steel toe - these are expensive and they can't get good construction jobs downtown without them - unfortunately, they are also often stolen!).

THANK YOU TO ALL!

My letter went off to my friends, and as interest came back, I formed a private Facebook group to coordinate the meal. It was titled "John's Meal" because John was the first homeless person Natalie spoke with who shared his story with her. And because I didn't know any homeless people, having a faceless John was perfect for me. I created a sign-up page for volunteers which I shared on Facebook. They could let me know if they would provide food, come and prepare it on Saturday, or if they would serve the meal on Sunday. By Tuesday, just two days after Natalie had served her big meal, she responded to me and our new group on Facebook.

Natalie:

February 23, 2016

I want to thank all of you for your heart and help! I have so much to share with all of you I don't even know where to start. I just want to thank Jen so much for taking the lead and organizing a group. It's this type of leadership I've been dreaming about for the last 6 weeks of doing this street ministry.

*In short, at the beginning of the year I read a book called "Under the Overpass" by Michael Yankoski. After reading, I felt a very strong conviction to step out of my comfort zone to help show the love of Christ. As a mom with young children, walking the streets of downtown Pittsburgh, volunteering in the emergency shelters at night, and feeding and carrying a heroin-addicted woman to safety is definitely "out of my comfort zone." **But I have been transformed.***

Over the last couple months, I've grown to love these people. I call them my friends (who happen to be homeless) and you will be amazed what a homeless man can teach you in an hour. I've been working with a woman from Mars named Christy and she created a public Facebook page called "Mission from Mars." Please like her page and posts and follow along. The more traffic she gets the more people we can reach. You can read about her and her story, but she is a single mom and nurse who has had a difficult journey through life. I am inspired by her and her heart to give back to the community that saved her.

For those of you that would like to serve on Sunday, Jen wanted me to share some lessons learned with all of you. I shared them with my

*core group that helped me last Sunday. But like the rest of you, I'm
learning along the way. Stay tuned! And if you have any questions
please comment, it helps us all learn!!*

Within hours, all the items needed to cook the meal were claimed
by volunteers! I was blown away by the generosity of my friends
and Facebook friends, who were volunteering to cook on Saturday
and then serve the meal on Sunday. While I had my reservations
about serving, I was excited. By the end of the day Tuesday, we
had everything we needed to make the meal for 100!

Jen:

February 23, 2016

*OK BIG WOW - we have everything we need for the meal prep on
Saturday! Thank you all so much! Looking forward to seeing some of
you Saturday and others on Sunday!*

In the background, Natalie coached us and told us more about
John.

Natalie:

February 23, 2016

*John was the first homeless man I met and he literally would not let
me leave. He had so much to say. He was your picture of a homeless
man – weathered, sun beaten face and hands, gnarly beard, worn
clothing.*

He is very private, but he taught me so much. He gave me so much information on my first day out on the streets and now 6 weeks later - I've seen it for myself.

During our talk he said, "Do you know what we need? Not what you think we need, but what we need?"

He said, "If you make this meal, you will get the homeless people out here that are not here for a tasty meal. They are here because they are not going to live through the winter. And you'll really have a crew of about 10 people that need ministered to."

The meal he requested: Bean and vegetable soup, no spices, no salt, bread and salad.

So, I gathered a group of people who expressed interest in helping the homeless and we cooked "John's Meal."

I met John when Mission from Mars first started street ministry about a month ago. There were only a few of us and a few homeless men and women sleeping on the corner. Last weekend we had 55 men/women out.

Natalie began to guide our small group with tips and pointers. She shared what it was like to serve people food on the street, where to go, how to interact. Most of us were completely terrified to go downtown to serve this meal, to stand outside in the freezing cold, to make ourselves vulnerable. The posts began with what to wear:

Natalie:

February 24, 2016

- What to wear: You may run into a situation where you may feel compelled to literally give the clothes off your own back. One week a man asked me for my backpack and I gave it to him. Another week a young girl was so cold and tired we had another donated jacket, but I would have left her with mine. I go with the mindset that I might feel so inclined to give, I might get back in my car with no shoes on.

- What not to wear: This is totally personal opinion, but I choose not to wear my rings or earrings. This, unfortunately, could create too much temptation. I do not allow my kids to wear 'school pride' apparel or sports clothing with their name on it. Because I do not know the backgrounds of the individuals we serve, I do not reveal many details about myself, contact information, etc. My kids once wanted to wear a non-Pittsburgh team sports jersey — we decided to change and not create any rival team riots!

As many in our group had children and wanted to know if we should/could bring them, a discussion about children also ensued:

Natalie:

February 24, 2016

Kids: Kids are welcome but it is at your own risk and your own discretion. I don't mean to worry anyone, but as a mom with children, this environment requires a close eye. When I've been down with my kids, it's been just us - they stick right with me and sit and talk with me. This past weekend was a new dynamic and when they go down with friends things tend to get more excited. And I love seeing their excitement to serve and give, but I did see a 10-year-old wander to an

isolated corner with a buddy to hand out socks. I will also send out
more on some discussions I've had with my group on prepping kids
before you go.

"What about giving money?" was a question on everyone's minds.
How could you not give? We have so much and they have so
little…

Natalie:

February 24, 2016

Be very careful about giving money. If you choose to spend time
talking with folks, you are going to hear unbelievable stories. You
might hear stories about how $15 will get them a bus pass to get to
work, or $30 will help them with a propane tank to stay warm.

This wasn't to say there aren't people telling the truth with
legitimate financial needs, but we didn't see ourselves as filling that
role. We had concerns that our money could be used for drugs,
which are a powerful enemy. We created an unofficial rule that we
wouldn't give money, but would give of our time instead.

Finally, discussions turned to photos. Natalie was adamant that the
privacy of the homeless was to be protected at all costs. What if
their families didn't know they were homeless? What if they were
fleeing abuse and the abusive partner found them from our
picture?

Natalie:

February 24, 2016

Pictures: You can take pictures but on behalf of Mission from Mars we ask that you do not take pictures of the homeless and/ or post any pictures of homeless on Facebook. There are some organizations that do this. But as we become true friends with some of these homeless men and women, they feel violated and used (their words). This is not a zoo and it is not just a drive-by charity event. We are here to show these people that **we are a community of people that love our neighbor.** *If you choose to 'document' this for your family, please be discreet and respect everyone's privacy. Keep in mind people have left their wives or husbands, some are teens and runaways, some have warrants. We do try to get a picture of the volunteers and post. And Christy from MFM asks for anyone uncomfortable to move from the picture she takes for the Facebook page.*

Any other questions - please comment!

As the day went on, the posts continued! Natalie gave more detail about her encounter with John and her sadness that he had not shown up for her meal on Sunday. Her family had questioned why John had not come to eat. After all, they had put a lot into making a meal especially for him.

Natalie:

February 24

Kids and teaching moments:

When we got home from John's meal, one of the kids asked me "Where was John?"

I haven't seen John since my original encounter early in January. At the time, it was just Christy and a few other people who came to drop off donations. There were just a few homeless men and women, maybe 8, mostly sitting around, sleeping in the park. That's when I witnessed men walking around with just two pairs of socks and no shoes.

Two weeks ago I wrote to John. I wanted to let him know I listened and I would be down to serve his meal – exactly like he asked. Another homeless friend found him and gave him the note. When John didn't show up, this became a great teaching moment and something I wish I realized better before we went down and could

have prepped families. But, like all journeys, often we learn along the way.

Having a large group of people serving the Sunday meal changed the dynamic of lunches in the park. In the past, it was Christy and a friend or two bringing a small amount of food for a handful or so people. Last Sunday, there were vast amounts of food, a large number of volunteers to serve, as well as a great number of kids. They were so excited to share their bags full of blessings, or to pass out socks, or coats, or anything else that we thought would be useful, but it was also a learning moment for our group. Kids rushing the homeless with bags of stuff, while well-intentioned, can create some chaos. It can also be intimidating for the people who were not comfortable with crowds.

Natalie:

February 24, 2016

Last Sunday was a good moment to reflect. I was thinking about our groups of kids rushing folks with toothbrushes, toothpaste, bags and shoes. It's a hard balance, but I think it's a good discussion to have with kids. It was so natural to be excited, but we also have to remember that whatever we do, it's important we remember to keep the focus on the people we are doing it for (versus our own good deeds) – that focus is often just connecting quietly and personally. A listening ear is often what these folks need most. The stories I've walked away with from just sitting have been priceless.

I love having the kids there, and I think it brings a wonderful spirit of community and awareness to our kids. And this is exactly what Christy wanted to create - a place for our community to come for fellowship.

As the discussions continued in our group, we tried to analyze what they "needed." Inevitably, our discussions surrounded material things we could not see living without, like dental hygiene. We couldn't imagine life without a toothbrush or toothpaste. We couldn't imagine not having a change of shoes or boots for when the ground is wet or snow covered. We couldn't imagine doing without a winter coat with the latest keep-you-warm technology. We were looking at the homeless through our own lens, but Natalie encouraged us to look at them through a different one.

Natalie:

February 24, 2016

Other discussion among friends:
- (I) totally feel you when you speak of discerning what they need. Rushing to "give"... food, clothing, toothbrushes... whatever, could actually be a deterrent. Ultimately, I believe "they" want to be loved, just the way they are. They want to know they are good enough and really, at the end of the day, equal to you or me.

Of all that had been discussed by Natalie, this point was hitting me the most. What they really need isn't toiletries or even food. What **they really need is someone to love them**, someone to talk with them, to care for them, and to feel like they can be friends. They desire to have people look at them with dignity and respect. Instead, many look down on them, feel pity for them, or ignore them altogether. I started to feel a tinge of guilt about my prior interactions with the homeless. Instead of looking them in the eye, I would have crossed the street and walked the other way.

Even with all of the preparations and desire to help, this was the first time I had thought about the homeless as something other than the homeless. I began to see them as people, with wants, needs and desires, just like me. As I became less afraid, they became people I wanted to meet and whose stories I wanted to hear. But, there was still a lot of fear.

It was so foreign, as if we would be encountering people from another planet that speak another language. We wanted the experience to be a good one for us, as well as for our kids. We wanted our young ones to learn and to want to help, but we also had a lot of trepidation.

Natalie's discussions continued, with talk of what it felt like to pass out the "stuff" we had collected, particularly from the kids' perspective. She told us how excited her own children were to be able to give and give freely. When they had opened the bag of coats and tote bags, it was like Santa was there with his elves! The excitement from the kiddos and the homeless was palpable; everyone felt like it was Christmas. The children felt good, and we began to devise strategies on how to better manage how to pass out "stuff." Maybe we could use a separate table; perhaps we could wrap the items in plastic to avoid handling and bed bugs. Another idea was that volunteers could simply hand the items directly to the homeless, to avoid many hands handling the articles.

There was so much information swirling about, including information about how to serve, what to serve, who to serve. What kids should and shouldn't do, how to avoid bedbugs. My mind was swimming. I was worried that what we were doing could not be replicated by a new group of volunteers, especially in such a short amount of time. Would anyone else be crazy enough to make the next week's meal? I had already begun to look ahead and badgered Natalie to share her information in a way that other people could follow. With all the messages and phone calls, we were spending the majority of our days figuring out how to make this work. But I knew that most people wouldn't consider helping us if it was difficult. We had to make it so easy that anyone could (and would) volunteer to make a meal for 100 homeless people.

Natalie:

February 24, 2016

Ok - Jen has convinced me to create a manual, with tips and tricks. For the longest time I wasn't even sure if anyone else wanted in on this journey I've been on. I've got much bigger plans and love having you come along as I navigate the trenches. Jen is already working on a "Cooking for Crowds" manual. Who would have thought? But in the meantime, hopefully you can navigate through my lessons learned series today. 1) Kids and dealing with mental illness 2) Clothing donations and 3) General FAQs.

I couldn't believe all that had happened in just a couple days! We had taken Natalie's meal and had begun to put a framework to it. We had manuals and FAQ's and lots of people were interested and excited to help. Natalie's stories had touched people. They wanted to hear more to find out how they could help. They loved the idea that their coat or donation would go directly to someone who was truly in need. It felt like we had so much to learn, and we had so many questions. We continued to pepper Natalie with them.

Natalie:

February 24, 2016

After we serve lunch on Sunday or down at the emergency shelter, do you wonder where these men and women go 'home?' Some will be able to get into missions, but due to a limited capacity and other reasons, others will be finding a spot on the street. Some have had their spot for years. Would you believe **some men sleep in port-a-potties** *at night and leave when the construction crew comes in the morning to work?*

The idea that some of the homeless were sleeping in potties sent me over the edge. I can't stand to be in a port-a-potty even for a minute, let alone sleep in one of those filthy, disgusting places! I was mortified!

As I tried to digest these sleeping arrangements, the conversations turned to drugs:

Natalie:

February 26, 2016

It's important that you also prep your kids to be careful about what to say and help them understand why... for both safety and the respect of the folks down there.

Just as an example - I overheard a conversation among kids. "Do you think they are on drugs?" Sometimes, most times, we cannot predict what our kids could possibly say... But something like this, heard by a vulnerable individual, could create a sensitive and possibly dangerous situation.

I love what my kids have learned through this experience and how we've connected as a family. And I'm glad I'm not shielding them from the realities of the world they live in, but I do want to make you all go in with eyes wide open.

If you have any questions - please comment or message me! There are no dumb questions.

And that was it. After those explanatory messages, we were now prepared to go out and help people we had never met and knew nothing about. Many of us had such nerves about going to serve, our stomachs were in knots.

Chapter 3

THE MEAL

"If you can't feed 100 people, feed just one."

Saint Mother Teresa of Calcutta

My husband, daughter, and I anxiously drove thirty minutes to the meal location, wondering what we would see and who we would encounter. Would we have enough food? Would the area be safe? We had a general idea where we were going, but passed the location three times. There was no indication that this was a place where people were being fed.

The location itself was outside an elementary school. The homeless mission is located directly across the street, and many of the homeless hang out in this park during the day. There were a few trees, a play structure, and some concrete. As our SUV pulled up with food and met the rest of our group, we saw a number of homeless people awaiting our arrival. There were probably around 40 people waiting, just standing around. I felt uneasy but not afraid.

As we exited our car, we were immediately greeted by Christy, the street minister Natalie had told us about. This was her mission, and we were excited to have a "professional" there to show us the ropes. She dispatched one of the homeless men to our car to help us unload, and we began setting up.

There was so much excitement surrounding our meal. The homeless community seemed so eager to see what we had brought and watched us with interest. Some were very shy and stayed away watching us from under a tree. Others engaged right away and offered quick thank you's and hellos. It felt welcoming from the start and immediately the anxiety level dissipated. Most of our suburban friends scarcely realized this community of people existed so close by, but almost immediately we could feel a connection building. We had met our first homeless people face to face, and I have to say they were different than I expected!

My first surprise was that some of them worked! Evander, our unofficial homeless liaison, was the picture of clean cut, and couldn't have been a better first introduction to the homeless. You would have never known he was homeless. He ran to my car to help us unload, set-up the tables and Sternos, got the line moving, and, I later found out, he was the one spreading the word on the streets and in the shelters about our meal. Evander had a dark brown face and thick, but short, black beard. He wore a beanie style black hat and had a huge, warm smile. He spoke with a bit of a drawl, which was even further disarming. I liked him from the first minute and so did everyone else, homeless and suburban alike.

In all of the subsequent times that I have met Evander, I have never ceased to be amazed by what an incredible person he is. He exudes such a gentle, quiet confidence and is a true leader in every sense. Evander lives in a shelter and works at a nearby canning plant. He doesn't work on the weekends, but isn't permitted inside the shelter during the day. So this guy who has been working hard all week is now stuck standing outside on weekends because he has nowhere else to go. He has no car or transportation. The madness of it is frustrating. No wonder so many homeless are depressed! It's the middle of winter and he can't go indoors? I know I have touched on this before, but meeting Evander and seeing the insanity of it was infuriating. I wished for a warm comfortable room with a couch and TV for Evander to relax and watch a game, rather than this bleak and cold park.

If I hadn't met Evander on the streets of Pittsburgh, I could have easily pictured him hanging out with my neighbors at a backyard party. He is articulate and well spoken. His clothing appeared baggy, but otherwise suitable, and he was showered and clean. My whole image of homelessness has been shattered by this one man.

How can he be homeless?

I was reeling from the thoughts, but I took my place in the food service line and tried to be nice. To smile.

As we began serving food, I didn't feel like I really connected with many people. I was so new and afraid. I was trying to act as though I wasn't intimidated, that I served homeless people outdoors on the sidewalk of an elementary school every day, but I am sure they saw through me. I kept a close watch on my girls, scolding them if they went more than a step away. They were so completely unfazed by the situation and the people they were meeting. They didn't seem to look at them any differently and were delighted to scoop pasta noodles onto their plates, eagerly doling out "you're welcomes" after the many grateful "thank you's" they received.

I, on the other hand, *was* completely fazed. Thankfully I was so bundled up, they could barely see my face and I could more easily hide my emotions and fears. While Evander was certainly neat, many were completely disheveled. One man's pants were stained and he reeked badly of urine. He begged me for another pair, but I had nothing to give.

I felt a deep sadness that rocked me to my core, knowing that **people** were living like this. They were so obviously hungry - the portion sizes for lunch were similar to what most football players would consume after a big game. And they asked for seconds, and thirds, and I am pretty sure one of the men ate 20 meatballs! We knew there were more people to feed in the camps, but didn't have the heart to turn away anyone that wanted more.

The conditions outside were cold and windy, and the temperature was in the mid-20s. I was freezing, but I couldn't help but think about how I was only standing in the cold for a short time, that it would continue to get colder as the day and night wore on, and they would have nowhere to get warm. I found out that some restaurants will not allow the homeless to stay and eat, even if they purchase a meal. Apparently McDonalds is homeless friendly, meaning they will allow them to stay and eat if they purchase food, so a gift card from there is a prized possession. Witnessing the hardships and struggles they bore on a daily basis bogged down my body like a weighted jacket.

When I came home and reflected with my family upon our service that day, it became clear to me that the service had changed not just me, but my husband and daughters as well. All had enjoyed the experience, and my daughters wanted to know when we were going back. I hadn't expected to go back again ever. I had cooked my meal and thought my obligation was over. But God had different plans.

After the meal service, I put some of my thoughts into words and shared them on Facebook. The experience affected me much more than I could have expected. I wanted to share it with the group who had donated the food, clothing, and blessing bags. I also wanted to thank them and allow them to share in the experience.

Jen:

February 28, 2016

Today we served the meal for Mission from Mars. Rewarding, eye opening, and even life changing are words that come to mind.

Met a guy whose 40th wedding anniversary would have been tomorrow. His wife left him, his son, now 18, he doesn't know. He's lived under a bridge for the past year. He's excited; he's going to be getting an apartment in three weeks. He's been robbed 7x this year. He wore 7 layers of clothing and was saving his money for a shave and haircut.

Another man seemed as with it as could be, clean cut, young. So polite - all of them. And thankful.

But this other man, he worked at a church and has worked construction. He starts a new job tomorrow. He's from Nevada and just wants to help people. Even in his current state, he can't wait to help the mission by giving back. Right now, he's taking Bibles to distribute to other homeless people. We all said grace together before the meal, and each of them was just so thankful. So thankful for the pair of socks or underwear we donated.

Or the woman we met who was newly homeless. Last week MFM set her up with everything she needed to live on the street, but it was all stolen from her this week. Everything. She had what she had on… and nothing more. Christy tried to get her into the missions this week (7 of them), but was unable. She begged for a tent and sleeping bag, but the ones we brought were already gone. The missions are out of both items.

It was a pretty incredible way to spend a day. If anyone has interest in getting involved in the future, let me know. It's pretty awe-inspiring watching God's work be done, and it was a very rewarding experience for my kids, who not only got to serve the meal, but also prepare it.

Thank you to the awesome people who served today, as well as all of the people who donated food, supplies, or helped make the meals. To say they were appreciated is an understatement. A bag filled with

granola bars, socks, toothpaste, etc. were received as if they were Christmas presents. Feeling grateful today.

While the meal was over, I couldn't shake the feelings of responsibility. My eyes were opened to this whole world of people in need and I felt like someone had to do something. I couldn't conceive that my meal would be the last. Yes, I knew that Christy would continue doing what she had been, but her resources appeared limited. You could see her heart was exploding with love for the people on the streets, but as a single mother of two, she was struggling to make ends meet. I began to feel more and more that this should continue, and our friends that helped make and serve the meal seemed willing to help out.

I immediately began recruiting my friends to make a meal for 100 people.

Wasn't this fun? You can do this too!

We encouraged the group within our private Facebook page. Amazingly, five people from my "homeless meal making party/group" said they would make a meal! Natalie and I began the process of mentoring our new volunteers.

Chapter 4

THE BIBLE PROJECT

"Blessed are they who hunger and thirst for righteousness, for they will be satisfied. Blessed are the merciful, for they will be shown mercy. Blessed are the clean of heart, for they will see God."

Matthew 5:6

One of the homeless men that we met that first week, Major, had worked as a Choir Director at a church out West. Details about his past were somewhat limited, but the story I heard was that he lost his job, was no longer able to pay child support, ended up in jail, and then homeless. I have no idea how many of these details are accurate, but this is what I was told. Now as you read this story I am sure you are thinking…what?

How?

More details please!

Is that really possible?

That's exactly what I was thinking.

I was beginning to find that the stories were always too short and never included all of the facts, details, or even relevant information. I became adept at sifting through and cobbling stories together, sometimes taking a tidbit that Natalie had learned and coupling it with a detail told to us by Christy. In any event, and in almost all cases, the details just never seemed to make sense. There is no linear trajectory that can explain how someone could have ended up in jail or on the street or both.

There were large gaps in information being conveyed, whether the person simply lost interest in telling us, had a drug issue that prevented it, or a new conversation or thing to do simply came along. It was not uncommon for someone in the middle of a story or conversation to simply stop talking to me. Being a newbie, I was far too nervous to push anyone, or question too far. So many stories became just snippets, pieces of a puzzle to later put together if I got to know the person further.

Major was a huge asset to Mission from Mars. Like Evander, he got the word out about the Sunday lunch and encouraged others to join. This younger man had dark skin and short, curly black hair. He did his best to stay clean even though it was extremely difficult. He had a neat appearance and was easy to talk with. Major had been sleeping on the ground with no blankets or cover, and we were thrilled that one of our sleeping bags had been allocated to him. He was excited about starting a new job, and even more excited to help Natalie pass out her colorful Bibles. His love of the Lord was evident.

Natalie is a faith filled person and probably the most evangelistic person I have ever met in my life. Sure, I had seen evangelistic preacher types on TV, but Natalie is different. Her faith is a part of her, and she exudes it in daily conversation. It doesn't come out in an overpowering "be like me" kind of way, rather, in the very matter of fact way she lives her life.

She is deeply rooted in her beliefs, and while accepting of others, she's also very aware of her call to bring others to God. Having not really known Natalie to this point, this was all news to me. Prior to chopping vegetables, we had a casual relationship through our children, now we were talking about faith, Bibles, and homelessness.

Natalie created what she termed The Bible Project after her early interactions with Christy and her first homeless service. The Bibles are decorated, for lack of a better term, in crafty, scrapbook style. She uses raffia tape (I had previously never even heard of it as I am most definitely not the crafty type!), highlighters, markers, pictures, cards, and bookmarks. You name it, she uses it. The idea is to make the Bibles readable and engaging for the homeless friends who receive them. By the time of my meal, The Bible Project was starting to get traction. A few Bibles had already been decorated and even delivered to those in the encampments.

Natalie describes how she got involved with the homeless and her special Bibles on her website:

> *"It all started with a potty. It was December 2015. Several things happened that I would soon realize were all part of God's plan. At the end of the year, I spent time in reflection and a devotional question resonated with me. "Are you willing to step out of your comfort zone to help show the love of Christ?"*
>
> *When I started to think about where I was uncomfortable, I was drawn to get involved with the homeless.*
>
> *I am not familiar or surrounded by individuals with addiction.*
>
> *I do not know much about mental illness.*
>
> *Some may (just may) call me a little germ-a-phobic (But I don't entirely feel like I qualify since I do believe eating week-old Cheez-Its off my van floor will boost your immunity.)*
>
> *I am not comfortable being in the dark, in the city.*

And to be completely honest – I'm very pragmatic. I do not usually side on the side of compassion; I'm more of a problem solver versus a hugger.

And quite frankly, everything about it made me feel uncomfortable.

So, I started my journey getting involved with the homeless. I researched missions, organizations and individuals who were serving the homeless.

CHRISTY

I came across a local woman named Christy. She was also new to this. But Christy was fearless. She was going under the bridges, in the alleys and into every corner helping the homeless, one by one. She wasn't with an organization and she didn't have a lot of money, but she had a huge heart. I would later learn her incredible survival story and her heart for the Lord.

Christy talked about "needs" for the homeless and one material problem caught my curiosity. There were middle-aged and older individuals climbing down snow-covered embankments to go to the bathroom. I was shocked and humbled and decided to take a huge leap of faith and buy a portable camping toilet on Amazon.

When I went downtown to drop off the potty and meet the homeless, I was confident a group of dedicated individuals could change the world. My eyes were opened very quickly with my first close encounter with the homeless.

THE FIRST HOMELESS WOMAN

Uncomfortable. That was me. There was a woman with eyes and cheeks sunken-in wearing no coat, shivering and throwing up in the sewer. She was coming off of a heroin high and unable to get a fix. I was pretty sure I was seeing her die right in front of my eyes. She lay right there on the street, hopeless. I tried to move her over to a cleaner

51

spot; she was shaking, weary and confused. When I asked her how I could help her, she said, "I just want to die."

And then I had to leave. I had to go pick up my kids and relieve my mother-in-law from babysitting. I went back to my warm, safe, comfortable house. But I couldn't sleep that night. Her face haunted me. Every night, I wanted to forget what I saw and just move onto somewhere else to invest my time and my mind. Some place where I thought I could help. I left confused. I didn't know what to do and my heart was heavy with no clarity. I was hesitant to give and help – was I enabling people? Was I making the problem worse? Would my donations turn into a crutch to not get off the streets? Would my money turn into drug money?

It was pretty clear God did not want me to look away. My days and nights were literally haunted by this young woman. What could I do?

THE BIBLE PROJECT

I felt the safest thing to do was to donate a Bible. So along with my potty, I wanted to send Christy with a Bible. But I was still worried; would it be used as firewood?

I thought if I invested time into the Bible by personalizing it, highlighting scriptures and writing notes, maybe someone would at least give it a chance and flip through it. I bought a small (4×6) Bible so it was easy to carry along in their plastic grocery bag filled with limited belongings. I started highlighting, adding flags, inserting bookmarks and post it notes with encouragement, hope, scripture and reminders of God's promises. I would pray intently over the Bible. It was so loved.

And off it went.

When Christy returned she told me the receiver had tears in his eyes. To receive something so personal and special it was a gift of more than God's Word. But it was a gift of His love. She said those around him wanted one too. And then I had a list of three.

After three, the list grew quickly to five and then ten and then I couldn't keep up. I didn't want to mass produce them, so I said, "one a week." And it still wasn't enough time.

I threw a cryptic Facebook post out to all my friends. I said – If you have a heart for the homeless and want to help me with something, let me know.

Once I pitched the Bible Project idea, I had two volunteers. Not even very close friends – actually one of my children's teachers and a soccer mom. I got them Bibles and they worked away.

Through the process I thought I was working on the Bibles to transform the receiver, but I left transformed. The quiet time I forced myself into allowed me to draw closer to Him, to sit in stillness, and recognize His voice. I felt the Holy Spirit stirring inside me and I felt my heart softening and growing in compassion. I felt His Grace, His Mercy, His Love. His Word spoke to me in such a new way. I was refreshed.

I thought – I must share this. And as I told my story of the Bible Project, more and more people have joined me. And I see God working in miraculous ways.

Fundamentally, we just work on one Bible at a time for one person at a time. Praying and trusting God to do the rest."

Natalie - The Bible Project Website

As part of a project within Natalie's church, she had received some funding to purchase Bibles. The project, termed the Kingdom Project, gifts $100 to individuals within their church to grow and build God's kingdom. Later in the year, another project came to fruition that benefited a homeless person through a Kingdom grant. A churchgoer created a portable pod-like shelter built from the material used for stick-in-the-ground type real estate signs. This plastic/cardboard mixture sign material was fashioned into the shape of a very small personal igloo.

The domed structure was about as long as a six foot tall man, with a height of about two and a half feet. If I had to sleep in it, I would think it might feel like a coffin, so claustrophobic and tight, but the recipient of this "castle" was moved beyond words to have such a sturdy structure to shield him from the harsh winter elements. I had never heard of a church incentivizing its flock to do for others in quite this way, and I loved the ideas it inspired. It seemed like pure genius to personalize the experience of serving others while motivating people to use their own resources, time, and energy to building God's kingdom.

The tiny house was delivered on a flatbed pick-up truck which rolled beneath the highway overpass. What a stark contrast the white igloo was to the shabby tents covered in blankets. It was partially hidden behind another tent to be less conspicuous lest an angry homeowner or walker of the nearby path would complain. It's a delicate balance in homeless encampment areas for the cities and communities surrounding them. No one wants the homeless to live in their backyard, but many also realize that they truly have no other place to go. It's a constant conflict between understanding the need and understanding the problems that can come with a homeless encampment, problems such as violence, drugs and alcohol abuse, among others.

Christy (MFM) in the igloo

Many people who work with the homeless advocate getting them off the streets and into shelter as quickly as possible. However, there are a large number of people who can't be accommodated by the shelters, or will not abide by the rules of the shelters; others won't go due to safety concerns. Even though they do their best to provide a safe and warm environment, there are stories of rampant bed bugs, rape (male and female), and theft. Many homeless feel safer outdoors than they do going inside.

It was with these people in mind that the igloo shelter was lovingly crafted, and there was so much excitement about its delivery. The homeless in the city encampment area were beginning to build a community, and that community was becoming connected to the suburban community through the igloo structure as well as the Bibles.

With Natalie's growing group of volunteers, Bibles were being decorated, but they needed a "man on the ground." This had to be someone who knew the homeless and could help find people who were open to receiving this special gift. Between Christy and Major, they had created a small network to deliver Bibles locally.

Natalie's small Bible project expanded quickly with many homeless requesting Bibles. At the meal service, Natalie gave out printed business cards directing those with needs to contact her via email (many homeless have phones or use library computers). To aid her volunteers, she began providing examples of how to decorate Bibles on her newly created Facebook page. The business cards were an easy way for the homeless to reach out to her and to request Bibles and prayer. As word spread, so did the requests, and they weren't all for Bibles. Many of the new emails that began to flood the inbox were for food or supplies.

Here's a message Natalie received to The Bible Project website from someone living on the streets:

Natalie:

March 1, 2016

> *"do you know where I can get some food that doesn't have to be refrigerated or heated to keep at my tent. i don't have time to chase down meals with work now. I'm wore slap out. plus I met this guy named Ray this morning who is homeless. 50 yrs old has seizures and mental and memory problem. say he gets a check and has 2 case workers but they won't help him get an appt and he's hooked on xxx. please pray for him."*

Always thinking and resourceful, Natalie then put out the following to our group:

Natalie:

March 1, 2016

IDEA! If anyone wants to do a 'drive' or gather some friends, I think this brings up a good idea. Create some sort of care package that has non-refrigerated/non-heat required meal options. Also have to keep in mind 'secure'/closed because of the mighty rats I hear about.

Let's back up...Rats! Literally, rats! The kind that can eat through tin cans, or coolers, or sleeping bags. Are you kidding me? I am now on the lookout for rat-proof foods that don't need refrigeration or heating? All that keeps coming to mind is: this can't be America. **I can't believe that people in America are sleeping on the road worrying about if rats will eat their canned goods!**

I wasn't ready to explore the seriousness of the problems we were encountering. At the same time, I felt I could continue to help by keeping the meals organized. Coming off the huge success of my meal (people arrived, ate, and Natalie didn't have to cancel her weekend plans), I was anointed my first title in our "fictitious" Facebook organization, which we renamed "Under the Overpass" (from John's Meal) in honor of the book that had inspired Natalie.

My new title, Catering Director, exemplified my willingness to manage the weekly meal calendar and ensure we had:

1. Meal hosts and

2. Volunteers to serve the meal.

Did I mention this was just a few days after I served for the first time and met my first homeless people? To give a perspective about how quickly things were happening, I've included the dates of some of our conversations. Things were happening at warp speed, as if time were standing still, so that we could catch up and help these people. Natalie and I had a discussion about just how much was happening and it seemed as though God was literally slowing down time to allow this work to be done.

Sometimes I think back to that initial meal in February, 2016, to this acceptance of these responsibilities, and I wonder if I would have done this any other year in my life. Likely not. But, leading up to my involvement in that first chopping experience, I felt like God was speaking directly to me.

It started on December 14, 2015. I was getting ready to make cookies with a friend when I experienced an allergic reaction. My eyes swelled shut, my nose felt full, and I felt a pain in my chest. The reactions continued, and eventually the pains got worse. After a few doctor visits, I was admitted to the hospital on February 4.

Those three days in the hospital were the lowest in my life. I was stuck in a world of pain and confusion. The doctors did not know the cause of my symptoms. I had a litany of tests, and my frustration grew. On December 13, I was basically healthy. By February 6, I was discussing all manner of specialists with my doctors.

To get through this challenging time, I was willing to do just about anything to take my mind off the tests and the waiting for results. When Natalie wanted help making her meal, I jumped at the chance to think about someone other than myself.

When I met the people on the streets, heard their stories and saw the badly scarred tongue of a man with seizures, I couldn't help but think how trivial my personal struggles were. This is when I started to believe that God had a plan for me if I was willing to accept it. I still struggle with the accepting part. It's not easy to make yourself powerless and vulnerable. It's not easy to put yourself in God's hands and say, "Thy will be done" and truly mean it.

Each day I struggle with this personally as I have my own desires - things I want to do. And, it's not always simple for me to see what God wants me to do. It's easy to get caught in a place of inactivity - a place where you're unsure, so you wait. You look for a sign to literally hit you over the head and tell you what to do, and then you still might not do it. At least that's how it feels for me. Each day I have to make that choice over and over again, and each day the choices become more difficult.

I wonder, if not faced with a serious medical issue, if I would have invested myself so fully. Would I have taken the time to organize, and give so much of myself to this team who were working behind the scenes in the Under the Overpass group to make life a little less bleak? Probably not. Likely God knew that too.

March was a complete blur. It was a whirlwind of planning, organizing, and feeding the masses, and I wasn't the only one feeling it. Even cool collected Natalie was feeling the energy and realizing we had to capitalize on the momentum. She continued quarterbacking for the Overpass group. It seems our entire local area had become involved in the ministry in some way, and she was determined to keep us moving.

Natalie:

March 3, 2016

Ok - I'm hiding for the next 3 days to get caught up and organized - we went from 8 to 50 (volunteers) in a month and my heart rate is exploding. I have a gazillion messages. How many people are in this town? I'm getting worried. HAHA. Everyone new - read the docs to get you started. We are set on the Sunday Lunch for the rest of the season! Jen - Catering VP just promoted from staff to manager to

*VP in the week, will help keep the Sunday Lunch crew afloat until I
at least take a shower. (Till end of May). Comment if you would like
a leadership role, hiring is hot at the executive levels.*

*I have more ideas and answers to questions I will make public soon.
And I should probably just have a happy hour for question
answering. Lisa - VP of Sous Chefs will provide the wine and
appetizers.*

*Go like Mission from Mars on Facebook to get the general updates
because I'm trying to get posts to Christy there first.*

*And - today's "Word on the Streets" - Man just got out of jail and
needs a home. Christy went to set him up. He will live in homes
provided by the Housing Director Rita and Jennifer C with donated
bus passes and bins of rat protected food, including rat poison. Name
is Bones and when I asked "Is he thin" it was "Because he breaks
them." Welcome to the team!*

So, a quick recap for anyone confused, just a few days after
meeting my first homeless friends, a few short weeks since even
hearing about Mission from Mars, I have now blown through a
number of fictitious titles (for real work I will say) including
Catering Director, Staff Manager, and now Catering VP. There
may have been more titles; Natalie was throwing them out so
quickly, I couldn't keep track. We had appointed a few new roles,
Lisa was appointed the Sous Chef, for her willingness to cook for
others. Rita and Jennifer, for their willingness to donate tents,
became our Housing Directors, and the organization was starting
to take shape. We had lots of people stepping up in a big way,
and as Natalie mentioned, we had "booked" every weekend from
March through May for food.

We couldn't believe the generosity of our friends and neighbors.
It was astonishing to see people who we may have known as a

soccer friend, or a bus stop acquaintance, becoming someone who we could talk with passionately. In sharing a common goal and working together, we began to see the good in one another. Hearts were exploding for something bigger than ourselves. It was unlike anything I had ever experienced, and I don't think Natalie had experienced it either. It was just so unexpected! Who would have thought that neighborhood moms would be driving a homeless movement? This group of disconnected people, many of us strangers or mere acquaintances, were talking and communicating multiple times each day plotting and planning for the food needs of the homeless, people most of us were still afraid of!

Even the fact that we were helping people with names like Bones, who probably quite literally broke them, could not deter us. We were people on a mission, and even if that mission was finding rat proof food containers, it felt good. It was tiring, but also invigorating. And it was really fun. It gave us an excuse to talk and get together, something we didn't ever spend enough time doing.

But there were times when it was emotionally difficult, especially when we considered the situation our homeless friends were enduring.

Natalie:

March 4, 2016

"News from the streets" - have you ever had the flu? One 50 year old woman, living under the bridge is sick. She's quarantined to her tent, and imagine.... No bathroom, no bed, in this weather........

People continued to take on greater responsibilities. They would see a need and seek to fill it, often while kids were at pre-school or during nap time. Our "executives" were mostly young moms at our best when multitasking. The organizational chart grew even further as Natalie helped Christy to outline a vision for what Mission from Mars could be in the future. My favorite part of the post below is that Natalie began encouraging people to submit their resumes! We laughed about how real our "fake" organization had become.

We were taking every bit of time and labor people offered and kept expanding the list of responsibilities for our group. I also got another quick promotion; I was now the Chief of Staff. Lisa added a new role, Luxury Goods Shopper, after she began finding special items for individual people, including a big and tall sized pair of pants. Our titles, and the work we were doing, were making us laugh and cry, sometimes at the same time.

Natalie:

March 3, 2016

Call me a liar - I'm back, showered and baby napping. Here's the executive Under the Overpass team. Feel free to use titles on your resumes. If you look at the job opportunities below and want to name yourself on the executive team (that's how the rest got here!), please submit your resume.

Jen - Chief of Staff and VP of Catering Operations. She will help with all Sunday meals.
Lisa - Executive Sous Chef and Luxury Goods Shopper
Allison and Jena- VPs of Special Services. When Christy needs something specific. Lisa is on your team.
Rita - VP of Housing. She was elected because she said she will get a truckload of tents and sleeping bags. She will keep inventory.

IMMEDIATE POSITION OPEN:
I need a VP of Donations (or whatever you want to call yourself!).

Job requirement: You are organized, can keep inventory, love to keep a clean closet.

I will need a 15 minute call with this person. I need this person to keep track of what we need and what we have coming in inventory. I will work directly with this person on what is needed to keep us stocked and what we are receiving from the MFM community page. This person needs to coordinate having the stuff organized and ready for storage (I'm not goodwill here!). This person will know the ins and outs of what we will and will not accept and why. For the time being, I will volunteer space to store (and may need a divorce lawyer because Rob is going to go NUTS). Is this you?

The clean closet was particularly important to Natalie, whose penchant for cleanliness is unrivaled. So concerned about bed bugs, insects, and just plain dirt and grime, she began packaging in clear plastic bags any items we would deliver. This served a couple of purposes. First, it served Natalie's desire to keep things sanitary; second, it provided an aesthetically pleasing way for people to receive donations from us. We wanted them to feel like the gifts they received from us where given with love, not given in lieu of throwing something away. These were our friends, and we couldn't give them junk, especially not with what they were going through. Many of our friends could only have but a few possessions, understanding that what they leave behind will likely be stolen. We wanted anything we gave to serve a purpose.

Natalie:

March 3, 2016

At the top of my iPhone FB (Facebook) page there is a link "Info" and "Files." If you are having trouble opening these documents, let me know. I'm trying to explore easier ways to follow and consume the general information versus the banter of a bunch of hyperactive women. But they made me laugh so hard today.

You are all doing fantastic things and love seeing the community come together as one! And new friendships formed, that's awesome!

We just got 2 more turkeys donated and as I ran outside to put them into the freezer in the MFM storage building; it was cold. So, think about our friends in the woods, under the bridge and 'living' in a 12 inch space between the road and parking garage tonight.

And here's a picture of my business partner's home for "The Bible Project." He is a college graduate who ran into some trouble; his wife left him with his kids and sued for a large sum of child support. He's not putting money toward a lease so he can pay his debt. He lives in the orange tent with the blue cooler. The food you are collecting will go in that cooler. The blankets you donate will go in that tent. He is distributing "The Bible Project" Bibles under THAT bridge. And he asks me for prayer, every single day to just get through tomorrow. And that is why we spent our day as we did. Thank you for joining me!

Homeless Camp under a Bridge

The people we were helping had a face. They had a name. They had a story. They had a family. They were asking us for prayer so that they could continue. They wanted hope that they could make it through one more cold night. That they could save enough to change their circumstances - that they could change their lives. Each and every one of us could relate. We could imagine running into a tough time and losing everything. What if we lost a job? What if we were sued and couldn't pay the debt? What-ifs swirling in our heads, we were being changed by the homeless. They began to look like people, like friends, like neighbors, and it kept us up at night.

Natalie:

March 4, 2016

My friends are sick under the bridge. I'm sending down frozen bone broth and put together a little bag. Gave me an idea! Sick Bags! I'm putting together a list, but if someone wants to pick up a 'donation drive' and get kids together to put these together, it's needed!

- Emergen-C packets
- Vitamin C drops
- Packets of Bacitracin ointment for cuts
- moleskin for blisters

Our friends were sick, weathering the cold frigid temperatures and battling common ailments we might have at home, like a cold or the flu, but without the many comforts we rely on to get ourselves through. If I have a cough, I grab the cough syrup. If I'm achy or feverish, I grab the Tylenol or Ibuprofen or both. Sore throat, grab a cough drop. Cut myself, put on some Neosporin and a Band Aid. All of these comforts are so readily accessible in my bathroom closet, but our friends had none of these comforts. Not only were they fighting colds and the flu, they had to contend with inadequate footwear causing terrible blisters and sores on their feet.

Foot sores can make walking any distance difficult and are worse in the winter when feet cannot properly dry. Imagine your shoes or boots (if you are lucky enough to have them), getting soaked with snow or rain. It's too cold to take them off, so you leave them on - day and night. They don't properly dry and neither do your feet. Even on your feet boots are not safe. I once heard about a man whose boots were stolen (from his feet) while he slept. Some of what we were hearing was unbelievable, but we knew much of it was true.

Natalie:

March 5, 2016

I want to thank everyone on this team for everything you are doing. Last night, Mission from Mars met a young woman on the streets outside of the emergency shelter. She is addicted to heroin and her kids have been taken away from her.

Thanks to all of you who are helping to support the many functions of MFM, she accepted help last night. She is ready for help and to get better. She will enter into a program for women who want off drugs and want to put their life back together. It is structured and strict, but they get help. She accepted. She accepted while our team gave out socks, tents, sleeping bags, and food. Without your help feeding these donations, she may have never stopped by.

So, thank you. These stories happen every day (and sad stories right beside them). But it is the effort of the community, non-profits, and passionate, loving people that will help each homeless person, one by one.

All jokes aside and make believe titles and org charts, thanks again for sharing your talents. Hopefully you realize by now, every talent and passion will fit into the big picture. If you don't know your talent or where you fit in on this journey, I will help you find it.

More to come, but a man we are partnering with sent me this today, "Is it not to share your food with the hungry and to provide the poor wanderer with shelter — when you see the naked, to clothe them, and not to turn away from your own flesh and blood."
Isaiah 58:7 NIV

Natalie and Christy decided to sketch out Christy's vision for the future and an umbrella of the homeless began to take shape. It included those under the bridges, in the alleyways, under overhangs, in the woods, in cardboard boxes, and on porches, all places we had encountered our new friends. There was the community component, which included friends, churches, neighborhoods, clubs, businesses, and The Bible Project. There were also the existing non-profits, the homeless missions, who were already in this space making a difference each day. Finally, God was at the center and heart of it all. There were a few quotes referenced from the Bible, inviting us to rejoice in the Lord and bring God glory. The vision was forming, and it became clear that Mission from Mars' mission was to connect them all: to connect the homeless to the community, as well as the non-profits, and especially connect them to God.

By the time Natalie sent out her next post, our tiny organization had expanded exponentially! She sent out yet another post defining our ever growing number of responsibilities, as well as our growing ranks of volunteers to fill them.

Natalie:

March 4, 2016

WHO's DOING WHAT (message or comment what I'm missing, I'm still adding to the list!!!)

Jen
- _Website designer and prototype_
- _Somehow trying to organize me_
- _Catering coordinator (creating menus, informing Sunday lunch volunteers, requesting bread/ desserts, who the heck knows what else I can't even keep up with her)_

Jana
- _Preschool donation drive and preschoolers assemble bags_
- _Making bone broth to freeze in quart size bags, labeled with date_

• *Making frozen quart size meals (chicken noodle soup) with cooking class*
• *Creating the Dept of Agriculture: Inquiring about setting up the 'giving garden' with graduate of gardening and possibly making 'garden pots' to deliver to camps*
• *Reading "A Shelter in Our Car" to students for awareness*

Michelle
• *Donation drive for Towels/blankets*
• *Donation drive at preschool*
• *Donation drive at elementary school*
• *Research on storage space*

Kristen
• *Donation drive for Towels/blankets*
• *Folding and packaging towels, blankets, coats and shoes! I LOVE HER.*

Rita
• *Inventory counter of tents and sleeping bags (since she buys a lot)*
• *Volunteer and sign-up coordinator for Sunday Lunch*
• *Donation drive for First Aid Kit and mini toothpaste*

Allison
• *200 comfort bags (did I get that right...200?)*
• *Backpack/bag drive*

Maddie•
•*First Aid Kit assembly•*
•*25 mixed snack/toiletry bags*
• *Children's reading buddy bags*

Lisa
• *Running her own Sous Chef kitchen with Allison*
• *Luxury goods coordinator – buying bras (I tried to tell her they are not necessary for survival)*

Jenene
• *Volunteer Spot assistant for Sunday Meal*

Tammy
• *Extra freezer*
• *Willing to massage homeless feet – obviously she hasn't been down there to talk about blisters…..*

GARAGE DONATORS
• *Lisa*
• *Michelle*

MAKING SUNDAY MEALS
• *Deanna*
• *Jennifer*
• *Susan*
• *Kristen*
• *Tammy*
• *Allison*
• *Tina*
• *Tracey*
• *Petra*

A flurry of posts continued. People were doing canned food drives and posting specials at local grocery stores. They picked up hams in bulk, and planned how to feed the masses deliciously and within a budget. They gathered to make delicious homemade cookies. And together on March 6, they again served with love.

Allison

March 6, 2016

Such a great morning!!!! LOVE!!!!

Tammy

Awesomeness!!!!!

Michelle

Well done my friends.

Natalie *You are all amazing and beautiful. For two weeks I haven't cooked on Saturday, felt pressured to get down there on Sunday and it's refreshing. And so weird, I missed it so much!!! But it's good to recharge after 6 busy weeks. Thanks for so many people making this your own and sharing your stories to inspire others!*

Jena *Volunteering and some of the gang made it into my daughter's nightly list of things that she is thankful for tonight. She said she was happy she got to go and help serve the meal, and that she got a hug from 'The Mailman' and a fist bump from Evander.*

Natalie *I love that!!! The one week I had to miss because I couldn't get a sitter for the little ones, I was so distressed I couldn't follow up, so I wrote cards to my homeless friends and sent them down with Christy. Will delivered for me and I called him The Mailman!*

Suzanne *Well done team!!! What a blessing you all are!*

Natalie:

March 6, 2016

So many things are going on, I can't even communicate it all out to you all, but this is from JUST THIS WEEKEND!

Great things are happening downtown on the North Side this morning/afternoon. Got a message from a homeless friend that folks were already lining up by 11 a.m. (for the 12 pm lunch)! The Foundation is down there shuttling people to haircuts and giving out free bus passes. Jen's off running to buy more food! I just got a call from a man at the car show saying they have pulled pork, mac n cheese and cookies left over and (asking) if I want them! Allison has 15 tote bags/ backpacks and winter gear for storage!

Tammy jumped on this moving train to offer storage and freezer space!!

My fridge has donated Girl Scout cookies! Jana just made bags of bone broth, and donated a ton of food and supplies! She is now in charge of the Dept. of Agriculture and working to help me with a long-term dream of having a giving garden at our house. We will be able to have kids and families help weed and grow and supply our Sunday Lunch efforts! Christy and I have a huge project underway - to be announced! The Bible Project was just picked up by a women's ministry retreat as their activity.

Wonderful things are happening in the community for our community. Be proud. If you are down serving today, comment on your day and share pictures!!!

The second week of our team coordinating and taking care of lunch for Mission from Mars had just finished up and by all accounts it was successful. We did run out of food, but only because there were so many people! I had run out to the grocery store to buy more food with another volunteer, which turned out to be much more complicated than you would think. Did you know there aren't very many grocery stores in the city?

When we ran out of food, I wanted to pick up something already prepared. I was envisioning driving to a market similar to my local grocery store, which is cavernous. There are more aisles than a church, and they go on forever. There are stations where you can have a pizza made while you wait, or you could pick up a freshly roasted chicken to go with your made-in-front-of-you sushi. There are shelves and refrigerated cases full of prepared foods ready to eat and enjoy. When I googled the nearest grocery store to the

North Side lunch spot, I was surprised to find it wasn't easy to pick up food for 25 people. I expected to stroll into the prepared foods section, pick up some sides, and leave.

The grocery store I found myself in was small. It was a little bigger than a convenience store, although not quite as big as the newer one near my house. We searched the store for hot sides and were quickly disappointed. We then went in search of cold sides. We fared marginally better in this area, finding only coleslaw. Dejected, we found some applesauce and headed back to the lunch spot, hoping our meager finds would be enough to feed the remaining people.

This moment of running out of food hit me deeply. In my house, if we ran out of food, we would simply go to the grocery store for more. But these hungry people couldn't simply open their pantry or refrigerator. They couldn't go buy more. The food we were giving them was all they had, and it didn't feel good to let them down. I resolved then that we wouldn't run out of food again, at least not on my watch. I couldn't bear to see the faces of disappointment.

The meal also underscored some additional needs in terms of donations. So few of us had ever done anything like this, it was important to pass along our accumulating knowledge. We continued to share the ever growing list of material needs with our growing group of volunteers, who were anxious to help.

Natalie:

March 4, 2016

DONATION DRIVE LIST: If you want to do a donation drive, these are the items we collect. Below is also a link from Mission from Mars for higher priced items - This is a list of items collected to maintain the encampment areas (where 3 or more tents are set up). You'll see comments as to why, for some unusual requests.

It is good for you to look at this list to also understand some of the needs. Like rat bait. We need lots of rat bait and bins to keep rats out.

(DISCLAIMER: You can collect 1) adult coats 2) adult gloves/hats/scarves 3) blankets 4) size 12 above shoes/boots/steel toed 5) used clean towels/washcloths. BUT YOU MUST CONSULT WITH ME FIRST. I have some 'rules' for the above due to lice, bedbugs, dust and that type of stuff and I am a Germaphobe. haha. (not really).

We would not take dirty, ratty towels, or anything that wasn't in good condition. And of course, what we did give away would be individually packaged in clear plastic bags, labeled with the name and size of the item. These small acts began to change perceptions within our group, and also showed the homeless that we cared about them as friends.

People (particularly newbies) in Under the Overpass were asking what they could donate and what the needs were. Natalie posted this list the same day and it became part of our "Reference Materials."

I should also explain what I meant by "donate." With a charity, you can drop something off at a physical location. Not being an organization, if someone collected an item, they would simply give it directly to a person in need or ask a friend from the group to deliver it on-site for them.

FIRST AID KIT
Q-tips
Snack bags (to put Q-tips or separate items in)
Quart size bags
Single use Bacitracin
Moleskin (for blisters)

...AND THIS IS HOW IT ENDS.

Cough drops
Zinc drops
Vitamin c drops
Chapstick
Antiseptic towels (individually packed)
Travel size lotion
Band-Aids, various sizes
Sting relief
Emergen-C packs

FEMININE BAGS
Single wipes
Pads
Tampons

NON-PERISHABLE BAGS/ BOX
Apple Sauce
Pudding cup
Protein drink
Protein bars, granola bars
Nuts
Single pack cereal
Instant milk – any brand

SUNDAY MEAL SUPPLIES
Forks
Spoons
Napkins
Plates (large)
Bottled Water
Chafing Dish Fuel
Half Steam Pans
Full Steam Pans
Lysol - any size
Hand sanitizer - any size

OTHER
Hand warmers

Mylar emergency blankets
Single wet wipes or small pack wet wipes
New Men's/Women's Socks
New Men's/Women's Underwear (large size)
Large black trash bags or 55 gallon drum liners
Mini/travel products: toothpaste, soaps, shampoos (save your hotel goodies!)
Quality toothbrushes, individually packaged (cheap ones – the bristles tend to fall out)
Sleeping Bags
Tents (any kind) – can be used

CHILD PACKS -
Small clear backpacks
Small beanie size stuffed animals
Thin Paperback books that fit in backpack (small)
Crayons
Coloring books
Or whatever you want to add that a little child may like and can fit in the backpack

PLEASE COMMENT BELOW IF YOU ARE DOING A DRIVE WITH A SCHOOL, CHURCH, FACEBOOK, AND GENERAL CATEGORY YOU ARE TARGETING.

Once we have a collection, I'll do a call for who wants to organize a group (great for kids) to pack up.

We had good Samaritans who were organizing collections at schools and within neighborhoods. Once the items were collected, additional volunteers would get together and sort the items into smaller bags to be distributed.

Natalie:

March 8, 2016

I apologize in advance that I don't always call out everyone doing great things. But when <u>Lisa</u>, Luxury Goods Coordinator, finds and purchases a 50 DDD bra and promises to get me a selfie.... then I just need to recognize her and let everyone know that she has been promoted to Luxury Goods Director.

If you're curious what else has been going on today with Christy and MFM, we were able to secure a practically blind man an eye appointment and contact lenses, and a donation of an exterminator to take care of a bed bug infestation. All in a day's work!

Not wanting to do more harm than good, we tried to become more knowledgeable about homelessness. We read books like *Toxic Charity* by Robert Lupton and Natalie summarized some of her views as well. Not being at all familiar with the homeless community or poverty alleviation, we were eager to learn. Our ranks had swelled to 75, and we realized we needed some common fundamentals to guide the volunteers.

Natalie:

March 10, 2016

I discussed today with several the importance of understanding how to alleviate poverty in order to make wise and sound decisions around ministering to them. I suggest reading the book "When Helping Hurts" if this interests you. But below are a couple key points from the book. We work closely with the larger organizations that understand and study how to approach homelessness in order to avoid common pitfalls but the goal, regardless if you are a believer, is to focus on:

Listening, loving and showing we care about them as human beings.

"Poverty is rooted in broken relationships, so the solution to poverty is rooted in the power of Jesus' death and resurrection to put all things into right relationship again. Jesus' work focuses on 'reconciliation."

Definition. "Poverty alleviation is the ministry of reconciliation: moving people closer to glorifying God by living in right relationship with God, with self, with others, and with the rest of creation."

"Reconciliation of relationships is the guiding compass for our poverty alleviation efforts...." **The goal is not to make the materially poor all over the world into middle-to-upper-class North Americans**, *a group characterized by high rates of divorce, sexual addiction, substance abuse, and mental illness.* **... The goal is to restore people to a full expression of humanness, to being what God created us all to be, people who glorify God...."**

"Poor people tend to describe their condition in terms of 'shame, inferiority, powerlessness, humiliation, fear, hopelessness, depression, social isolation, and voicelessness.' The mismatch between our perceptions and theirs can be devastating for relief efforts. Solutions must go beyond the material. We devise our strategies based on our understanding of the causes. If we misdiagnose, we likely do harm.

If we think the cause is lack of knowledge, we will educate. If we think it is oppression, we will work for social justice. If we think it is their sins, we will disciple. If we think the cause is lack of resources, we will give them resources. The underlying diseases are not always clear. And the people themselves may not always know or be completely honest with themselves. A sound diagnosis may lead to a very long, time-consuming solution."

The book that Natalie references here, *When Helping Hurts* by Corbett and Fikkert, was just what I needed to read. I was struggling with the internal conflict of potentially enabling or making problems worse, but felt unable to turn my back to very real physical needs. The books we were reading, and the points Natalie highlighted, helped me to craft my own views on poverty alleviation, realizing that much thought had to be put into every donation we made and every interaction we had. I didn't want to do anything that would make their situation worse.

As a child, I was warned not to feed wild animals or they could lose their ability to fend for themselves. While we would never want to apply this sort of thinking to people, it made me think that we had to be conscious about doing for people what they could do for themselves. We had to allow them to keep their dignity. Sometimes this meant stepping aside to encourage self-sufficiency. Having Evander and the others help unload cars and take out the trash allowed them to contribute to our lunches as equal participants. Our group became conscious of the term "hand up" rather than "handout." We tried to inspire people to give of themselves, rather than focus on the material possessions they were receiving.

Natalie:

March 9, 2016

When asked what to bring, just bring yourself. The greatest gift we can give the homeless is our time and heart and just listen. The most important thing is that we do not want them to see you as someone who can meet their material needs. They need to see you as someone who can meet their emotional and spiritual needs.

As much as I/We want to help people, I believe we have to leave room for God to work. If being homeless ever becomes more comfortable than living in a home, we have not helped them. The key is to provide a hand up, but not a hand out.

Core team will be talking about this, donations and more! Stay tuned!

Our astonishing growth in numbers within Under the Overpass necessitated the creation of a smaller core team to handle leadership and organization. It became unwieldy to have all of our discussions with close to 100 people. It's important to note that Mission from Mars, the public Facebook entity that Christy created, was also growing by leaps and bounds. Her work was being seen and noticed by others, and our group stayed behind the scenes quietly fulfilling needs for Mission from Mars.

Given Christy's history of health problems, we were fiercely protective of her and her time. While it frustrated her, the Under the Overpass group was a closed group run by Natalie and myself, and Christy was not involved behind the scenes. She was bombarded by requests from the homeless at all hours of the day and night and we knew that the litany of questions and requests within Overpass would overwhelm her. I think this may have bothered her initially, but she was grateful for our help and support. I also think she realized we had her best interests at heart.

While Natalie and Christy created visions for connecting communities, I worked directly with Christy on developing a web presence. We were still not a non-profit, rather strangers coming together each week. There were new volunteers coming to serve each week, many who had never met before, so it seemed important to have a public reference point for new people.

As we kept learning and growing together a frequent conversation topic was, "What do I say when I meet the homeless?" It felt like we had nothing in common, and it was at times hard to get the ball rolling. We didn't want to accidentally say anything that would offend. We also had to be conscious to not give out too much information about ourselves, our families, or where we lived. There was always a feeling of danger in not knowing anything about the people we were meeting, not knowing their pasts.

Natalie:

March 12, 2016

WONDERING WHAT TO SAY WHEN YOU TALK WITH THE HOMELESS???

I loaned out my copy of "When Helping Hurts" but one of the things I learned from it was an idea of what not to say (and what to say). In short:

"Don't ask - What do you need (what they do not have)? Focus on asking - What are your gifts? What are you really good at? (what they do have)."

I focus conversation on this a lot. The premise is to not focus on what they do not have, but what they do have and how they can turn that gift back into the community.

Look at your involvement with this community - I promise when you recognize your gift, you will find such joy in being able to share it (even when you thought you might not have time, energy, or money). I see the gifts of shopping, cooking, gardening, baking, organizing, writing, folding, planning, leading, inspiring, ministering, and more coming out day by day from our group.

I love this discussion of individual giftedness. If I asked 100 adults what they are really great at, or even good at, many would say nothing. They believe there is nothing special about them or their gifts. They think others could do things as well or better than they do, minimizing their accomplishments and abilities. This is so hard for me to accept, as each person has been given gifts and talents, given uniquely for a purpose. Finding those talents, and even the purpose, is part of the tremendous blessing and fun in our lives! It's that feeling of flow when we are doing something we enjoy, when work ceases to be work because we are in the zone doing it.

The incredible thing about our group was that people were finding what they were great at, even if it was in small roles. They were inspiring and cooking, baking, and organizing. But even better than the use of individual talent was the collective talent that was evolving.

On our new website we wrote, *"Never doubt that a small group of thoughtful, committed citizens can change the world. Indeed, it is the only thing that ever has."* This quote from author Margaret Mead was just perfect for our group. Our team had commitment, and people were pouring their time and energy into it. They were passionate and their kindness was spreading like wildfire. It seemed as though the entire town was ablaze with the spirit of that kindness. Have you ever heard that one draft horse can pull 8,000 pounds, but two can pull three times that number (not double), 24,000 pounds! That was what it was like in our group. The more horses we added, the more work we could do. We were multiplying our work not by the amount a single person could do, but by some extreme multiplier effect where working together we could do and accomplish so much more.

Kelly:

March 13, 2016

God is so good!
As some of us drove downtown today to serve our new friends it was raining. We set up tents over the food just as God shined His light down upon everyone there with the sun. Tiny drizzles didn't start again until we were leaving. God is good all the time, especially today.

*As Max and I set out today to be blessings to others serving food
with amazing families in the community, I never expected to receive so
many blessings as I drove away. The feelings of nervousness and
anxiousness I had driving down immediately disappeared with hellos
from our new friends - that is, friends from the community whom I
"know of but don't know well" and friends from the city. Teenagers
and classmates my children go to school with that I typically see on
sport fields or down school halls, so graciously and willingly jumped in
and helped with not an eye rolled nor hesitation. What wonderful role
models my sons have in our community to look up to!*

*A man felt blessed by what we were doing and started reciting Psalm
23. I was familiar with it, but didn't know it by heart. Thankfully,
I had brought a tiny Bible in my jacket pocket that I pulled out and
he asked me to read it with him. And so we did. Another man was
in pain from the loss of his sister a few months ago and his father last
week. When he started talking about "God" and the path he is
spiraling down from sadness, I asked if I could pray over him. He
allowed me. God's wonders prepared my mind and heart from a
women's retreat at my church this weekend for these two situations
through conversation and God's love.*

*Watching kids (and adults) just want to give and serve walking
around to the steps where our new friends were eating, just pouring
out the extra food and filling grocery bags of all the goodies brought
smiles and genuine feelings of thankfulness to both those receiving and
giving.*

*I think what the "coolest thing" I experienced today was when people
asked "What church were we from?" I could proudly reply, "We
aren't from a specific church. We go to church. But in fact, we are all
families that simply have come together in our community preparing
food together and bringing it down to share with all of you." The
smiles they had knowing we did this "just because" warmed the heart.*

Thank you Natalie for bringing the attention to our community the need that is out there for the homeless right in our backyards. Although we think we are able to bring blessings to others (and we do), it is the blessings bestowed upon us that we receive by giving that continue to make us proud.

Chapter 5

THE PRESENTATION

"When we give cheerfully and accept gratefully, everyone is blessed."

Maya Angelou

When we bring items to the meal such as clothing, hats, gloves, we try to be careful about how we present them. We want the items we give to be neatly folded and laundered. To be clean, something we would give to a friend. We made this an unofficial policy because of Jerry's story.

It was Jerry's first day on the streets. Literally. Jerry has a college degree and had been working as a social worker. He had lived with his girlfriend, and her kicking him out coincided with the loss of his job. To my knowledge, Jerry does not have any addictions, but he has had some really terrible luck. Jerry came to us after his first very long night of being homeless. He had slept in the train station with his bag, praying no one realized he had nowhere to go. He found a baggage tag on the ground, attached it to his bag and acted like he was waiting for the train. He slept little and was very restless. In his eyes you could see desperation and fear. Christy had seen him on the streets, told him about our meal and he had come. He told Christy about his job interview the next day and she had promised him a shirt.

The things we take for granted the most - things like fresh laundry, are the things that make getting out of the cycle of homelessness so difficult. Jerry had a job interview the following day, but he had nowhere to clean up, nowhere to sleep, and no fresh clothes to change into. The shelters were full. Christy took him to the back of her worn minivan and began looking for items for him. A tent and a sleeping bag were promised, although she didn't have any with her. She offered to take him to "camp" (an area with several homeless living under a highway overpass), where at least he wouldn't be alone.

We pulled a rumpled, white collared dress shirt from the trunk of Christy's car. Jerry was thankful to get it, but I looked at the shirt in horror.

You're going to wear that shirt to a job interview?

I immediately had visions of Jerry being stopped at the door, being told to turn around, the shirt being too big and wrinkled to even be allowed in the door! Christy apologized profusely and offered to take it home that night, iron it, and bring it back out to him at the campsite. The fact that there are people in the world like Christy that would even offer to do such a thing is remarkable to me! She has a true servant's heart.

Jerry simply thanked her for the shirt, told her it would be ok. She directed him to a public shower facility, and he disappeared with his new, wrinkled shirt...for his job interview.

Jerry didn't get the job and I blamed the wrinkled shirt. Christy took him to the encampment area, where he "moved in" under the overpass.

Many in the Mission from Mars community were saddened by Jerry's circumstances and wanted to help him. Jerry's story was a great example of the community coming together to do something special.

A business owner heard Jerry's story, and hired him to work at his restaurant. He even had a staff person pick him up from the camp until he was able to get his own transportation to work. Jerry was now working hard, 50-60 hour weeks to get back on his feet and save enough money for an apartment. He was incredibly motivated and was a great employee.

Finally after a few weeks, Jerry had saved enough money and found an apartment. He made an appointment with the landlord for noon that day. As I said, Jerry had been working long hours in a restaurant kitchen, and he was exhausted. Jerry fell asleep at the campsite for an hour before meeting the landlord. When Jerry woke up, he had been robbed. The $500 in his pocket was gone, along with his apartment.

This story was so heartbreaking! Here was a guy, maybe 25 years old, trying to make something of his life, trying to get off the street, who just kept getting kicked back down! But Jerry persevered. He continued working at the restaurant, continued living at the camp, and by the next week he had enough money for his apartment. He moved in, and instead of never looking back, he met me a following week at the encampment area with food for the homeless living there.

The restaurant owner that hired him had given him food to take back to the homeless camp. The change in Jerry was palpable. His confidence was back, he held his head high, and he seemed to be almost in awe of what had happened. Just four short weeks before, he himself had been homeless. Now he was providing food to the same camp in which he had lived! And although Jerry's confidence was back, it was an easy confidence, a smile, a laugh, not a boastful swagger. Jerry knows just how perilously close we all are to homelessness, and I doubt he will ever lose that fear.

As we finished another week of service, the weather began to change, and we were beginning to see a light at the end of the cold,

Pittsburgh winter. We began to think more about fellowship than about material things. We had decided that our meal service would end in May, feeling we would have covered the harsh winter months and most difficult time of year for the homeless. While rewarding, the ministry was also tiring for our volunteers, who were coordinating, cooking, and providing for many each week. Natalie shared our news with the Under the Overpass group:

Natalie:

March 14, 2016

OPPORTUNITY! As we move into spring, our goal moves from survival (material goods, clothing, blankets, hats coats, etc) to community building. Folks on the street will have a much easier time now that the weather has broken. We will resume fall and winter focusing on the material needs. We want to use our time on Sunday for fellowship lunch and an activity.

IDEA: I'm looking for someone that would like to coordinate and help lead this sometime April 1 to May 31. Some sort of 'art' or painting project. Once I get a leader, we will assemble a volunteer team. Whatever we can do cost effective - posters, watercolor paper, etc, paint, paint brushes. And just paint! After lunch, we do our paint project, which will help us to talk and do something together.

THINK OF MORE IDEAS LIKE THIS! Please share other ideas as we approach spring and it's a little more comfortable outside.

Seeing this post compelled Gigi to get more involved and to use her artistic gifts. She's a mom like me and many of the others in our small Facebook group. Prior to her introduction by a neighbor who had chopped vegetables at Natalie's, she had no involvement with the homeless. Like many in the group, she had heard stories about the community that was building downtown and decided she wanted to be a part of it.

Gigi is in direct sales, and she decided to donate a portion of her income to helping the homeless through this event.

As she began to plan and purchase items for the art project, Gigi and I began to interact and a new friendship developed. She joined our core team, and immediately began using her many talents and skills to make a difference in creative ways.

Little did we know just how "creative" some of our friends would be when we hosted our first ever Suburban Families Paint Panhandling Signs With the Homeless Outside in the Park event; I mean, Art in the Park. The planning began for this new and fun event, but before we knew it, the Easter holiday was upon us. Our painting project would have to wait until after the holiday.

Chapter 6

EASTER

"We all possess God-given talents. No one can claim to be so poor that they have nothing to offer others."

Pope Francis

On Easter Sunday, our homeless friends came out to see us and one another. More than one remarked that they had been looking forward to this all week. This meal on the sidewalk, rain or shine, cold or warm - how could this be the highlight of anyone's week? My family came straight from church with nothing, just brought ourselves as we had been doing often. It was gratifying that the homeless who gathered had food to eat, a special meal that was prepared with care just for them with true loving hands. But what touched me most that day was when I talked to Will, Evander's best friend.

I asked Will tentatively, "What will you do with the rest of your Easter?"

He replied, "I had my Easter here with you today. Couldn't have asked for anything else. Today was perfect."

He went on, "I just like getting to see the people all here together, and appreciate that you would come down to the city to spend Easter with us."

Will shared a common residence with Evander, a shelter nearby.
Also like Evander, his enthusiasm and smile were contagious. He
was so immediately disarming, making you feel right at home when
you would talk to him. He made it seem normal to hang out on a
sidewalk, talking and eating on the street in the dead of winter.
With Will, it actually did seem normal. We wanted to come out to
see him and our other friends, just as they wanted to see us. Will
became one of my favorite homeless friends and the only one with
whom we ever shared our phone number.

I don't condone sharing personal information with strangers,
particularly the homeless, but by this point, Will wasn't a stranger.
We had gotten to know him and to really consider him a friend.
He was great at teasing me and the other volunteers, offering us
tips on how to loosen up. He might say, "I promise not to bite" or
silly little phrases that made us realize the distance we were keeping
from our friends at lunch. I have gained so much from the
homeless, but one of the biggest things is to be open to
recognizing what we can learn, regardless of someone's appearance
or status. The great blessings they can bestow upon us, from their
enthusiastic laughter or their optimistic spirit, many of the
homeless shared these traits with me in abundance.

It's not always easy to open ourselves up to learn from others, and
to do so from the homeless can be particularly humbling. What
could they possibly teach me? What gifts could they possibly share
with me? What do they have that I don't have?

If we can open ourselves to that vulnerability, we can see the
remarkable gifts and talents they can share with us. It has never
been easier for me to see God than through my homeless friends.
Through their incredible faith, their exceptional fortitude and
courage, and through their sheer will and determination to live, I
have witnessed a strength and character rarely witnessed in my
suburban surroundings. I have seen selflessness and self-sacrifice,

courage, and perseverance the likes of which I had never seen before.

They were giving as a sacrifice, not from one's excess, but giving from subsistence.

When we begin to listen, to see the homeless as people God created, it changes how we think. It changes how we answer questions about child predators and even murderers. It can be easy to provide compassion and care to those we love, to those who are sweet and innocent, but not so easy to love the unlovable.

Whether it's physical repulsion, for their bad smell or lack of teeth or hygiene, or whether it's their past that repulses us, meeting people in homeless ministry makes you look at things through a different lens. It allows you to view people in a more compassionate, forgiving, and merciful way. While it is easy to judge the convict for their past crimes and transgressions, it is much harder to forgive. When we acknowledge the convict as what they are, a human being, it changes perspectives and can even change people.

Here was my post to the group that day:

Jen:

March 27, 2016

We had a great day to serve today. Beautiful weather and lots of happy people. Will's excited to be starting a new job Monday at Bread Company. He couldn't wait to find out our favorite bread so he could hook us up! All of the regulars were there and then some. Probably about 50, plus the camps. Then another 20 or so came after we had run out of food. Unfortunately, 2 families came after we were done serving, all we had left was dessert. This was very sad, *young kids with them. One was the same girl from the other week with her grandma, but the number of kids had multiplied.*

For future meals, think we need to try to overdo the mains and skimp on the dessert portion. Most don't eat it. We might be better off to have peanut butter crackers, nuts, fruit bars, fresh fruit, etc. Or cookies as they seem to go much more than cakes.

I think a part of our issue in running out today was that the portions they are taking are much larger than normal. Also, many are taking food to-go.

Another thought is to bring juices as well as water when we can.

Serving today on Easter was a humbling experience. They were asking me what I had planned, what I was doing later. It made me think of all the food our family will have. I asked them what their plans were. Not one had any past our meal. Our meal was Easter for them. We had some awesome live music, courtesy of our formerly homeless friend "Cowboy." I felt privileged to be a part of it. Thank you all for what you contributed to our Easter celebration.

Chapter 7

STREET DELIVERY

"No one has ever become poor by giving."

Helen Keller

You want me to do what?

You want me to go where?

The answer came from Natalie, "Go out on the streets and into the camps…"

Are you serious?

Natalie:

March 31, 2016

Who in this group is interested in street outreach? In other words, who feels comfortable, who is willing, who is passionate, who is curious, in not only serving on Sundays but understanding how you can better meet the social and emotional needs of those folks we meet.

I am working with LIVING Ministries and other organizations who service the homeless community in a small group education forum/mentoring guidance in the early fall. I'm curious to know who would be interested from this group.

There is no obligation to actually do the street outreach, more if you are interested in knowing more about the dynamics, tips, lessons learned, questions (such as, a woman said she was a rape victim while on the streets....what do we do... or, this man is a heroin addict and told me he wanted help....). This doesn't call you to be a social worker - just an informed and knowledgeable volunteer!

The idea of learning about true street outreach set in for many within our group. And we continued to learn more about what life was like in the camps.

How do they go to the bathroom?

Where do they go?

Before the Luggable Loo, there weren't any facilities to speak of.

Natalie shared a link:

March 29, 2016

You probably haven't noticed where the boys and I sneak off to go to the bathroom at soccer games, but if you doubt me being germ cautious, I have one of these in my van. LOL. Hot summer days at a ball field, port-a-potty, yeah, no.

I received a cash donation this week from one of you - thank you. I bought 2 of these for women in tents on your behalf. These 2 women struggle physically to make it to any public bathroom.

(Link to "Luggable Loo" portable toilet- looked more like a 5 gallon bucket to me!).

As the weeks and months went on, we became more comfortable with those we were meeting. We enjoyed going to lunch and serving, and we were invited to participate in a new role with Mission from Mars, street delivery. Christy and Bonnie would typically pack up leftovers after lunch and bring them to the homeless camp, or directly to those on the streets. She asked us to join her.

The first time I gave out meals on the street, I was terrified. The fear was similar to the first day I served, but so much worse. Christy had suggested we help with street delivery before, but we always declined. We were certainly not ready for whatever "street delivery" or homeless camp delivery entailed. Christy continued to encourage us and made it seem like it was required now that we had become so much more involved in the mission. She wanted us to see where the leftover food went and wanted us to meet her friends who lived in the homeless camp under the bridge, people we had been hearing so much about.

We had begun to develop a friendship and relationship with Christy, and she really appreciated our help. She was so thankful that we had organized friends to keep the food coming, and she worked diligently on the streets and on social media to ensure people knew about the lunches. She was so passionate, so full of vigor for these friends who happened to be homeless. She wanted to help them so much, and we wanted to help her.

When her friend was unable to drive for street delivery, Joe, my husband, and I decided to go with her. This wasn't planned, but Christy needed a driver and had asked Joe. I wasn't about to let him go alone, not that I would provide any protection, but I knew I would worry until he got back. Plus, even though I was cautious and afraid, I was also excited. I wanted to see what it was like and where she went. I was curious to see where all these homeless people were hiding. I certainly never noticed them, so I had no idea how she was simply going to go and find them.

We loaded to-go meal containers into the SUV and started driving the streets of Pittsburgh in search of homeless people. Yes, you heard that right. We literally drove down the street looking for homeless people. But homeless people don't always look homeless, which is why Christy's trained eye was so important. The people we often drive by or walk by, the faceless people on the street that exist in the shadows, these are the ones we were now looking for. We would approach someone, often with a small backpack or grocery style bag, and Christy would ask them if they were hungry. Even writing this down, I still can't believe that we were driving down the street in search of homeless people.

Whatever illusions I had about street ministry were debunked as we drove around Pittsburgh's North Side and downtown. I had expected they would be in set locations that we would be delivering to, but as I would soon learn the homeless are often forced to move along. Armed with 25 to-go containers, we hit the streets. We were ready to feed the hungry!

Our first stop, and I mean a literal screech-the-tires-to-a-halt stop, was for a pair of young guys around 20 years old. They were clean cut, wore jeans, and each carried a small backpack. Backpacks and grocery store bags are often telltale signs of the homeless, but they can also be signs of students, so it is important to look for other clues. This is all according to Christy, our guide. She's so wise in all things "street."

As we drove down the road, we looked for people with bags and certain characteristics, like the absence of jewelry, beat-up shoes, and multiple layers of clothing. We had learned that the homeless can carry very little, so the more they can layer they will. I once met a man with 20 layers on. He was as big as a lineman and could have easily played in the NFL, or at least that's what he looked like with his many layers. Every article of clothing he owned was on his person, so that he had to carry very little and could also stay as warm as possible.

So, we wondered, now that we've found our first homeless people, how on earth do we approach them? Christy had her ways, and I think God must give her the words. She didn't know this pair of kids, and she simply asked them if they had eaten today. When they put their heads down in an embarrassed way, she quickly started her story with a smile.

"We're here making days for the homeless…and in this container I've got the most delicious meal you've ever eaten. It's a true Pittsburgh special, kielbasa and sauerkraut, some pasta, and there might even be a Danish in there."

You could see their faces light up and the sparkle return to their eyes. The boys told Christy they had not eaten in days. They had come to Pittsburgh on a train from Atlanta.

"Train jumpers can be fleeing abuse," I am told by Christy. "Some are runaways. Some have come in search of a job, and others are simply looking for adventure so they hop on a train."

The problem for many train jumpers is they often don't know where they are headed and are quite unprepared for the conditions they will encounter. I once met a train jumper, likely around 18, who had on flip flops in the snow. She had come from Charlotte, and it was warm when she left. It was below freezing with snow on the ground when she arrived here, on the wrong train. She had no money and nothing to change into. When I met her, she was dressed for summer as the snow was falling. Those types of encounters were the ones that made me throw hand warmers and a coat I was willing to part with in the trunk of my car, just-in-case items for the ones who really needed them.

Another jumper told me he did an internet search to decide where to go. I asked him why he chose Pittsburgh, and his reply intrigued me.

"I googled all the big cities and was looking for the greatest number of available high paying jobs. And so I jumped on a train and headed to Pittsburgh. I'm here looking for a good job to get off the streets."

The first day of street delivery is still very clear in my mind. The most difficult to see among the people we met that day was a man of about 55. He was disheveled and freezing.

We came upon the man after mistaking another man for being homeless (yes, it's as embarrassing as you would think to ask someone if they are homeless and hungry, and for them to tell you they live in a $5,000/month condo); but, that encounter led us to the broken man on the street. Undeterred by her blunder, Christy asked the man from the expensive condo if he had seen anyone he thought could use our help. He told us he had just passed a man on the street who appeared to be close to death. We turned the SUV around and headed back in search of our man.

Before we found him, we came across two guys in obvious need of our help. We stopped and talked with the men, who were so grateful for the food containers we handed them. I learned then that this was a prime location for the homeless to sleep and try to get warm, as the sewer system below ground warms this particular spot. I wish I were kidding, but I am not. So this North Side location is popular during the weekends (when the store is closed), but is deserted during the week when the store is open.

After giving the men food and our only sleeping bag, we left. They were so grateful! They had piled cardboard boxes on the ground as protection, but the cold weather was having an obvious effect. Christy gave out information about the Sunday lunch and invited them to join us next week. We then moved along in search of the other man, who we quickly found about a block away.

We approached the broken man very cautiously. He appeared to be in and out of sleep or consciousness as he sat on the step in front of a closed business. It was a very cold day, low-20's with a brutal, whipping wind. He had a coat, but no gloves. His salt and pepper gray beard was covered in tiny icicles from where his own breath had collected. The man looked at us in confusion when we offered him food. He didn't remember when he had last eaten. Christy tried to ask him for details, like where he stayed, but he looked around blankly and just said, "Around."

"Do you have a sleeping bag," he asked her?

We told him no. Christy had just given our last sleeping bag to the man we met just minutes earlier.

I wished for a sleeping bag or a place that would be open to buy one, but none existed nearby.

The broken man was very difficult to converse with. He seemed to know we were there, but had difficulty sustaining a conversation and even staying awake. I wanted to ask him a million questions, I wanted to take him inside, and I wanted to make sure he was ok, but instead he simply nodded off while we were talking to him and we walked away, back to our warm car.

I barely closed the car door before breaking down in tears. I searched through my glove box for anything more I could give this man, a granola bar, hand warmers, anything. I found a couple small items and returned to him. He thanked me, and nodded back to sleep. I returned to the car again, but this time I was the one that was broken. The way this man was living, if you could call it that, was more than I could take. It was too heartbreaking, too difficult to see or even understand.

All of my past fears about the homeless, all of my past wonders about whether or not they had done something that led them to this place, none of it mattered to me anymore. It didn't matter to me if he had done something to deserve this fate. I couldn't fathom that prisoners living in solitary confinement were living a more difficult life than the man I had just met.

My core ached for this man. My soul ached in a way it had never ached, not even in the death of loved ones. This one man with the ice covered beard, this man who could barely open his eyes and was literally freezing, changed me. My vision was no longer of a homeless man lying in front of me. **All I could see was a person who was hurting. A person who was struggling to survive. A person who was all alone.** There was absolutely nothing I could give this man that would have any real impact. It was at that moment that I really understood what Natalie was doing with the Bibles.

There was only one person who could help him, and it wasn't me. The only one who could handle problems this big was God. It was a humbling experience to feel completely and totally helpless, completely out of control. God opened my eyes wider through that experience. He showed me that there are issues bigger than me, things that no human can fix. Within our culture, we certainly can attempt to bring people inside and eradicate homelessness if we choose, but there is nothing we ourselves can do to fix the brokenness inside each of us. That healing needs to come through God.

Sometimes I think back to that man, that experience, and I wonder, could we have done more?

Should we have taken him somewhere?

But where? The shelters were full. Would he have even considered getting into the car with us (likely not; he had barely even acknowledged us)? A hospital? The options were limited. The fact is, it's not safe to put a barely coherent person you don't know in your car.

It made me appreciate even more the missions that make their facilities available for those who need them, however limited their capacity. For all of the rules and restrictions that the missions place on people, I also understand the reasoning for the rules. It would ruin all chances for success if someone is using or dealing drugs inside the shelter. But when you are faced with a person like the broken man we just met, whether or not he is using drugs doesn't seem to matter. Rules seem to matter even less.

How could a person ever hope to become clean while living on the streets freezing? I never would have considered this question before encountering freezing people who were also possibly using drugs, but now that I have, a quick one-size-fits-all answer isn't enough. For me, it comes down to something very complicated.

Should we allow someone using drugs to enter a homeless shelter? Short answer: no. They might bring drugs into the shelter, possibly damaging other addicts' hopes for recovery as well as creating a volatile and potentially unsafe culture. There are so many reasons why the answer should be no.

But...and there is always a "but" when considering the homeless, how is someone who is sleeping outdoors in the middle of winter expected to fight addiction, fight temptation under these circumstances?

I think about all of the times I have tried to diet, and how difficult it can be at certain times of the year. I think of Christmas cookies and birthday parties and times when you just can't quite stick to it. If I am this weak about desserts, would I have any hope of breaking a drug addiction while sleeping on a concrete sidewalk? A place where there are no supports to lean on, instead many temptations. At the end of the day, if you're homeless and have $5 in your pocket, you can make a choice (yes, heroin can be found for as little as $5). You can buy a value meal at McDonald's or buy a heroin high. Choosing that high may temporarily take them away from their misery - a short escape from their drab reality. When you really weigh the obstacles to getting clean and off drugs on the street, you realize just how much of a struggle it would be.

So what is the answer? Where should these homeless people go? What should we as a society do for them, if anything?

These are legitimate questions to wrestle with because even if you want to help someone, there is a point where people must want to help themselves. They might have to hit rock bottom. They have to want to come clean for themselves.

Natalie and I have had many discussions about this topic, mostly because when you are helping the homeless, invariably you have to decide how to draw the line related to support. Where is that line? Will you give food, but not clothing? Food and clothing, but not tents or sleeping bags? How do you feel about giving pots to help them heat food over a fire, or wooden pallets for firewood, or to keep their belongings off the ground? What about a cooler to keep food cold and keep it from spoiling? Are you making life so comfortable under a bridge that people no longer try to assimilate into society, won't seek the help of the shelters, or won't come clean?

Ministering to the homeless is a unique challenge. The questions raised by meeting them, hearing their stories, and considering the ethical dilemmas compound the ministry.

While there are uplifting highs when you feel you are really making a difference, there are the awful lows, where you feel guilt that PEOPLE are living as they are. And just when you tell yourself you can't do it anymore, you don't want to go back, you no longer want to see or feel their pain, they motivate you and offer you lessons. They make you think and consider "loving others as you love yourself" in a whole new way.

Below is my post after the experience.

Jen:

April 3, 2016

Another awesome day of serving- and stories! So a huge shout-out to Allison's team who had enough food to feed 200 people! We were able to feed all those in attendance as well as both camps (approx. 20 people), plus we fed lots of people downtown through street delivery. We are paying forward some silverware and kielbasa as well!

This week had a different feel. Many of our homeless friends had to choose today between our meal and their job on a Sunday, which for many is panhandling. I learned that Steelers fans are very generous and many were praying that Pirates fans are as well. Last night was very hard on some of them. The look on Yvonne's face when I told her we had coffee - priceless. She said I had no idea what that meant to her, she had been having such a bad night.

She didn't know how she was going to keep going on. Yvonne has been homeless for a year and a half. She lives in one of the camps under a bridge. She's one of those who chose the meal today rather than panhandling, although she seemed to second guess her decision more than once. Yvonne's face bears the burden of living outdoors. I have met her a few times, but only today connected with her. Last night was cold and they didn't have any hand warmers left at the camp. She was up most of the night. Yvonne chose to come to MFM today because she wanted to see her friends - Christy and Bonnie and the whole gang!

The winds were whipping last night, and Virginia (another from camp) told me that one gust was so hard that it propelled her almost over the edge of the camp (she was in a tent at the time!). The wind whipped and the snow fell, and *she was very cold as well. Her hair showed the toll the night had taken on her, even though we stopped after 2 pm. Virginia had always looked cleaner and put together in past meetings.*

I saw Major and a few others from Camp 2, who are now completely out of plates and cups. They could really use some plastic bins. Camp 1 was in much better shape and sported the new paper igloo (no idea what to call it) that was donated. It is a funky looking structure! Both camps had plenty of firewood. Camp 1 had a grill grate they cook over and even some tarps to shield the wind. I was amazed to see that the camp is actually right next to the bike trail for all to see and pass by. The other camp is more hidden, but still under a bridge. Camp 1 is very clean and we saw all of their clean dishes which were drying!

But for those of you who are still with me in my stories, I need to share what touched me most today. It wasn't having conversations about the Pirates, Final Four, or Trump (although I did all with our friends and enjoyed it). It wasn't seeing the camps, although that was certainly eye opening. No - it was doing street ministry with Christy. When Christy asked Joe and I to deliver to the streets and camps with her, I wanted to, but had reservations. I had no idea what I was going to see or find or if I was prepared for it.

Our first few deliveries were literally guys standing on the street. Maybe with a sign (only a couple), but mostly just guys Christy would see walking and ask if they had eaten today. She had about a 75-80 percent success rate on who she pegged as homeless/ not homeless.

So - we approached people, asked them if they were hungry and told them we were there to make their day. I actually think we made quite a few days today. If you ever want to feel like you are really helping someone, I highly recommend this experience.

Two men and a couple things stood out in this story. On more than one occasion, we were told of a friend who hadn't eaten, who they would share their meal with later. Thankfully, Allison's crew had made so much, we were able to fill both bellies!

Man 1 - We met a guy by Beauty Supply. The street is heated here through grates, so lots of homeless stay in this area. He was sleeping in a doorway, had some cardboard under him and a small thin blanket. He looked like he was FREEZING! Christy talked to him, gave him meals for him (and a friend, who we later saw and he thanked us profusely) and Christy asked if he had anything else. No sleeping bag. Christy promised one to him and we brought it back later. The joy that we saw was awesome. He immediately jumped into it with a huge smile.

Man 2 - The next man we saw was in really bad shape. His head was in his hands and his beard was full of frozen spittle and leftover crumbs. He had no bag or extra clothing. He said he had not eaten. This was the most difficult situation I have seen with MFM. You could tell the time outdoors with no protection from the elements was hitting him in full. He didn't complain, but seemed almost detached from the world. This was true suffering. We did not have another sleeping bag to give out. I ran back to the car and grabbed the last container of food and a few hand warmers from my glove box. It was all I could do and it broke my heart. I brushed away tears as we headed back.

We did a lot of good today. YOU ALL did a lot of good today. Those who provided Sternos (Bridget) and hand warmers (<u>Rita</u>) and the many, many people who donated blessing bags and food today- you did a lot of good and helped a lot of people. Thank you!

Deanna: I saw you guys as we were heading to Pirate game. It gave me such a warm feeling to know that something very special was going on over there!!

Kristen: You guys amaze me week after week! Jen, thanks for sharing your experiences and being so brave. I'm not sure I have that bravery yet.

Michelle: Thanks for sharing. You guys are so full of love and warmth to so many people.

Laura: Beautiful Jen. Thanks for sharing! I love these updates for those of us who don't go every Sunday. Do you feel there is a need for something specific? Sleeping bags/blankets?

Tammy: Thank you SO much for sharing!! It's so good to know that every last bit of food went to people who truly, truly needed it. I imagine these are only a few of the stories of what you experienced today! I look forward to meeting you in person.

Kelly: Thank you for sharing this Jen. Wow! Seeing Christy's posts this weekend and reading this makes it oh so even more real than what we even see on Sundays. Tears fill my eyes reading this as I'm getting ready to put on my warm pajamas. So thankful...

Alaina: I can't wait to dive in. I am thankful for being able to help in any way possible!! After seeing/reading everything everyone has dedicated, gone through, and how many testimonies have been posted on here, we are so

*grateful for what we have and ready to help and serve others
any way we can!!*

Joanne: *I continue to Pray for All involved in this
Special Ministry...*

Suzanne: *Jen – thank you so much for sharing.
Humbling stories that touch on our heartstrings. Such
good people doing such extraordinary efforts. Great job
everyone!*

Tammy: *If you knew how God could use your
suffering—if you understood the heavenly "cash" you
possess in your suffering—you would lose your fear and
would actually embrace it, for even your very offering has
been redeemed.*

*Read this today. Great reminder for this group and this
mission. Happy Friday!*

Natalie:

April 8, 2016

*Just got done pumping gas. Those 3 minutes were bone chilling cold
and it's April! Reminds me of our dear friends - with no emergency
shelters to go to tonight. It breaks my heart.*

*(The Emergency Shelters were no longer an option, as it was past the
"winter" season when they are open. Unfortunately, no one told that
to our weather!)*

*It reminds me of the first day I went down and I met John and Amy
(who so many of you have befriended through her ups and down and
moods), but also of the man who showed up with three pairs of socks
on, wet. He had no shoes and he was so excited for new socks. And
the woman who was about 65 years old, with no coat on a day like*

today. We didn't have a coat and the mission didn't have her size. I was crushed. I went and bought a coat for her but we never saw her again. I carried that coat weekly for 6 weeks hopeful. But never found her.

Homelessness is not a problem. So many of you have joined me in learning it's not a problem. It's a person.

Thanks again to all of you for sharing your hearts. I've seen a transformation in the feel and images of the folks on Sunday from January to now. They are leaving happy and looking forward to us. We now have tables! We have coffee! They are getting up and taking showers, getting haircuts and brushing their teeth!

You are helping them by your presence assimilate back into society. This is a huge step in the right direction and an incredible outcome of Sunday Lunch. Bravo!

Of all the words Natalie posted, the ones that really have stuck with me are: **Homelessness is not a problem. It's a person.** When you see the homeless as a problem, it's easy to come up with solutions to eradicate it. Put them in shelters. Clear out the encampment areas. Tell them to get a job. It's all very easy when you think of them as a problem. A problem by its very nature begs for solutions.

When you see the homeless as human beings, as someone experiencing turmoil in their life, clinging to their only possessions in a grocery bag, you might feel less compelled to make them pick up their sleeping bag and move on. You might begin to develop some compassion, even if you still want them to find a job or get indoors.

As my time with the homeless has increased, so has my empathy. I have thought about what a typical day might look like based upon stories I have heard and compiled from our friends. Below is an example scenario one of our friends may have encountered:

I wake up achy, still exhausted from my sleepless night. The noise of the train overhead and passing traffic occasionally disturb my slumber. I never fully succumb to sleep, fearful that if I do I will awake to my possessions being taken - the boots being removed from my feet. I need those boots, tomorrow I will interview for a construction job, and without them I can't start. These boots cost more than I will make in an entire day's work.

I wake up determined to get the job. Unfortunately, I don't have a watch or a way to tell time, so I have to estimate. Some of us have phones, but have nowhere to charge them. We call them Obama phones (because they are funded through a government program), but they rarely meet our needs. They are supposed to allow us to communicate with potential employers, but with little or no data or texting allowances, communication is difficult.

I wake up with the sun and realize I smell. I slept in the only clothing I have. There is a shower facility, but it's about five miles away. I begin the walk, taking care to avoid the puddles of melting snow, trying not to get my boots wet. My blisters ache and I long to take off my shoes and socks, but when I arrive at the facility, I cannot leave them outside of the shower for fear that they will be stolen. I once heard a man say he would cut my leg off for my boots. I believed that he would.

The shower feels amazing, but without soap and shampoo I don't get as clean as I would have liked. Some people gave me a bag of toiletry items, but it was too heavy to carry. Now I wish I had them or some deodorant to freshen up.

I am excited for the construction job. It should be a good payday, but now I have to get there. It's a 10 mile walk from the shower, and I sense I am running out of time. I hurriedly put on my clothing, knowing that the smell is not what I would like, but my senses have become dull. I don't really notice the odor anymore. I wish I could brush my teeth. I can't shake that feeling of sticky dry mouth. I haven't eaten this morning and I won't until dinner at the shelter. I was fortunate to have a good dinner last night, and I hope it will sustain me today.

As I walk to my interview, I begin to sweat. I am wearing all of my possessions and am now warming up. Not my fingers or toes, just my core, which is covered by 3 thick layers. My feet still ache, but I trudge on. I arrive at the site, excited to finally make a decent wage. The site manager takes one look at me, my appearance, and decides not to hire me.

Dejected, I make my way back to the camp. Hours have passed and I have walked many miles. I have eaten nothing. I still smell and my feet ache even more. I fall asleep and pray.

As the cold weather wore on, so did the hardships. The winter months take a toll on a body constantly exposed to the elements and the need for medical attention is heightened.

Natalie:

April 8, 2016

The woman Christy had been spoon feeding was hospitalized this week for pneumonia. She was just released per her insistence so she could panhandle on the corner. Christy is headed down with bone broth made by the wonderfully cute kids at the preschool and Jana!

Panhandling. Even the word used to make me cringe. The idea of holding a pan or any other object on the side of the road to collect money just hit me the wrong way.

I thought, why are these people just sitting there doing nothing all day, asking me for my hard-earned money.

I would cross the street to avoid their eyes, as if looking at them would somehow force me to empty my wallet. Of course, I assumed that in emptying my wallet, I would be robbed, mugged, or murdered. **I didn't see a person. I saw a problem.**

Christy decided to panhandle one day to see what it was really like. To see how easy (or difficult) it would be to make a living on the street. She dressed down in sweats and sat on the corner with a sign. After hours of "flying the sign," Christy had earned very little money. She was cold, hungry, and every ounce of her body ached. She gained a newfound appreciation for the endurance involved in panhandling.

Why panhandle? Why not get a job? It just isn't as simple as it sounds.

Jen:

April 10, 2016

Sundays have become a really special day for our family. Today we met and served 67 people - a new record at our service site. Additionally, we served 26 in the streets, plus 20 or so in the camps. That didn't count seconds - we had a lot of food! I think the really cold temps brought them out, but also the word seems to be spreading. The raffle was a fun addition! And in case you were wondering, yes - that is a lot of food!

Joe and Connor did street delivery on their own this week, Christy hung back with me. Her back was really hurting, and I could see her slow a bit.

The idea of my husband stopping homeless people on the streets to offer them food amazes me. He shared a couple stories of people who remembered us (Christy and I) from last week. They found a few people hanging out near the warm spot at Beauty Supply again. On a cold day like today, I wonder if this is the only thing that's keeping them from freezing.

A lot of the guys shared tips on how they stayed warm today. It was awesome to witness how our community has sprung fellowship among our homeless friends and also our community. Today was probably the most interaction I have seen between the homeless and also between homeless/helpers.

Homeless Blanket Tip: In case you are wondering, the blanket layers below you must be greater than or equal to what's on top - otherwise, you will lose your warmth!

Another cool effect of our community has been to make it difficult to distinguish the homeless from the non-homeless. I love this about the group, because it reflects that we are all equal in God's eyes. It also helps remind me that any one of us could fall on hard times, and I would like to think someone would help lift us back up!

Today was personally disappointing to me as our families (with children) didn't come back. I had saved some food for them and stuffed animals and Bonnie had brought some canned foods to fill their bellies. But, God brought us a couple new people that needed us more. I had been hesitant to close up shop waiting for our families that come after church. At that moment, two new women showed up. One had been released from jail on Thursday. She was in her early 20s, and her eyelids were puffy and swollen from crying. The woman who was with her said someone had seen them crying and directed them to us. They were sheltering in a bus pavilion not far from us. The older woman said she had a home, but was more often in the street due to an abusive home situation.

She saw the younger girl and took her under her wing, "I have daughters and would hope someone would look out for them if they ever needed it," she told me. Our young friend was wearing sandals and had on a thin coat. She had nowhere to go, was cold and was scared. They both couldn't stop telling me how they felt God had put us together. Gigi and Kelly's team immediately outfitted her with new boots and a warm coat! And we sent her away with dinner, snacks and some fruit. I can't thank Gigi and Kelly enough for what their team did today! They fed so many (with food to spare!) and provided some boots and coats to some people that really needed them! Hats, gloves, granola, water, you name it, this crew had it all!

And the stuffed animals - one went to the right home. One of our young girls in camp took a My Little Pony doll. She couldn't stop combing its hair and holding onto it, Joe said she was absolutely transfixed. If you are young, scared and living on the street, a stuffed animal to hug might just be a big deal. Yvonne told me she has one too (in camp).

A couple needs that came up this week - XL size sweatpants for a man with a urine bag that leaks on his pants. AA batteries for another man who likes to listen to the radio. And one final prayer request...for a man who isn't ready to quit drinking, but who I pray will get there soon.

He's a sweet guy who is reeling from the loss of his mom about 3 months ago. He keeps himself clean at the Wellspring showers and is a proud guy looking for work. But he is battling addiction and was in jail not long ago. Pray for inner strength for him to overcome his addiction and get his life on track. Also pray for healing as he deals with the loss of his mom.

Finally, Sky's will be taking 2 weeks off and we need Overpass group to be there to guide our new folks. Please message me if you can go next week, new or old! I have some extra granola bars and stuff to give you for next week.

Gigi: *So blessed to have helped so many. Thank you for all of our generous, kind, hardworking neighbors and friends!*

Tammy:

April 24, 2016

So today...wow. Simply amazing. You ALL are touching so many LIVES!! I truly believe the motto for this group should be--- homelessness is a person, not a problem. For real. I met these people today and was humbled and in awe of everything I saw and everyone I met. I "walked the line" today and spoke with countless homeless men, women and children. Some were happy just to have a handshake and a smile. I gave away NUMEROUS hugs :) And I witnessed such fellowship among all of our homeless friends as well as those who volunteered. I must admit - I was nervous before this weekend---how will we have enough food for all of these people? Will the food be any good? Will I feel comfortable enough to serve and socialize with everyone? All of my fears immediately were put to rest today as soon as Connor came over to my van and said--hey! Thanks for coming! And the rest is history. We had an awesome group of volunteers who pitched in and made this all come together. Each and every contribution--be it time, money, donations, prayer, etc.--all came together in such a beautiful way on such a beautiful day to serve our friends.

Some highlights--I met a group of three people I call "Three's Company"--a guy AJ, his girlfriend Stardust and their friend Allie, all newly homeless. They arrived later in the afternoon, and luckily Christy had a bunch of to-go containers still in her van, so we were able to feed them. We stocked them up with granola bars, paper towels, baby wipes---they were so appreciative of anything we could provide. Just released from prison, they are trying to navigate the streets and figure out how to survive. AJ has food allergies and therefore is very limited in what he can eat. He was so hungry, saying he hadn't eaten in days. I told these three to stick together, and that there are people who are praying for them, and that things will look up. I told them I would pray for them by name, and they really seemed to take to that.

I met another woman who saw me hugging Bonnie goodbye, and she yelled---hey! can't I get a hug over here? Well, of course! I gave her a huge hug. She never met my eyes, but I can't help but think maybe that was the only kind gesture she had received in a long time.

And I met a man in line waiting for food who actually apologized to me because he said he smells and his pants were soiled.

The art--SO COOL!! This really provided an opportunity for everyone to just "be" and enjoy each other's company....no worries about food, or comfort, or where they are going to sleep or go to next. Just having fun and conversing. This along with other opportunities for everyone to hang out and just have fun should be a staple with this group!

Some ideas/observances:

-BANANAS and ORANGES! These went SO fast. Fruit to hand out that they can take with them is key. Bananas were especially asked for among those with children.

-BABY WIPES - I was asked by several for these. I was able to get some from what someone had brought to serve, and I got some from my car as well. I'm going to send some down with Christy next week, but these could be a staple in our various drives. I watched a man literally take his socks off and wipe off his feet with the baby wipes I gave him and he told me--you have no idea how good this feels.

-COFFEE - We didn't have any today, thinking this wouldn't be necessary on a warmer day like today. The very first people I encountered said--where's the coffee?? You guys always have coffee!! I felt so bad...we should consider trying to have some every week if possible.

-THERE IS NEVER TOO MUCH FOOD!--soooooo true. Even though I felt like we cooked and cooked and cooked all weekend, we could've had even more. I don't feel as though we "ran

out" since we were still able to take some to the camps, but I still wanted to give more!

-Smiles and handshakes go a LONG way---I could see how happy people were when I just went up to them, shook their hands and told them my name. It was awesome. Some even started calling me "T" and it made me feel so included in their world.

That's about it from my small piece of the pie. Thanks to Natalie and Jen and Christy for all of your support, advice and encouragement to get me hooked on riding this train! I can't wait to serve again, and will be thinking of my new friends tonight :)

Jen: *Tammy your stories here are awesome! I am so excited that you got to share this experience and really feel it in the way that I and many others have. So excited you are ready to jump in as a concierge- you will be great!*

Natalie: *I read it beginning to end and loved every bit of your reflection. Welcome. You will never be able to look back, you're on the train and will be dying to go again.*

Cynthia: *Great stories Tammy. Love reading these every week. Can't wait to help out again when my family can.*

There were so many affirmations swirling around the group, so much gratitude that they had been included. It was Tammy's first service, but you would have never known. She was completely at ease with the homeless, so thoroughly open to sharing the infinite love that permeates every one of her pores. She was hugging and smiling, I was in complete awe of her ability to easily communicate. She was made for this ministry for sure!

Many of us were on the lookout for lice and bedbugs and were so careful with our touch, but not Tammy. She gave the warmest bear hug to all who would take them, never once thinking of hygiene, sanitation, or safety. She was a tremendous asset to our mission, and eventually took on a much larger role within our core team.

Chapter 8

ART IN THE PARK

__To Fly The Sign__- Homeless lingo describing the act of using a sign for panhandling. Also known as flying a sign.

After Natalie posted her idea for Art in the Park project, there was a whirlwind of activity surrounding what to do and what to bring. Gigi compiled a simple Wish List for the project, and she posted it to our group. People in our Under the Overpass group could help by contributing supplies or offering their time to help. The homeless were also getting excited. We found quite a few were talented in the art department.

Panhandling Sign Read: Need Weed

Natalie:

March 28, 2016

Here's some 'artwork' a homeless friend was working on yesterday – designing his panhandling sign. (excuse the Need Weed message...)

The first ever Mission from Mars "Art in the Park" is scheduled for April 24th following the meal. Meal time 11:30 – 1:30. Art around 1ish or when we see people starting to finish up. Gigi has a passion for art therapy and volunteered to coordinate and lead! If you would like to help 'sponsor' this event, please see the below list of items needed.

If this is something you want to be involved in, let me know.

Art in the Park was our way of bringing some enjoyment to the homeless meal. It was a way to provide non-material fellowship and to help our friends focus on something fun for a brief time. On April 24, 2016 we had over 100 homeless turn out to design and create with us after our regular Sunday lunch. Gigi and Christy brought supplies. The volunteers joked beforehand about what kinds of art would be made.

Would they only come to make panhandling signs? Yes, some did, but the majority used the opportunity to create something that was theirs. The creative, but not as appropriate, "Need Weed" sign was not replicated at our event.

When the festivities began, some very colorful characters came to join us. Diva was a delight to meet. She had never been to any of our homeless meals, but she was excited to join us that day. When she saw the clothing that someone brought out, she immediately grabbed a shirt and gave me a huge hug, much to my surprise.

"Girl, I just had to hug someone!" she told me.

I invited her to stick around to paint with us.

Diva is the epitome of a gregarious woman. She was stuffed into her tight fitting college branded clothing with a bright red braid of hair perched on top of her head. Her smile was big, her laughter was bigger, and she was hard to miss in the crowd. She grabbed a large canvas from the table and began to paint. When I came back later, I found a beautiful masterpiece on her canvas. She had splashed abstract ribbons of black, red and gold onto her white canvas. The pride on her face beamed brightly.

She was so thrilled to have created this art with us and was thanking me profusely.

"I'm gonna put this on my living room wall, right in the middle, when I get my apartment. I want my place to be decorated in these colors, red, black and gold, so that's why I used 'dem. Someday I'm gonna have my own place and I'm gonna hang this right up, girl, you know it!"

She teared up a little, "Girl, I am gonna hang this in my place."

Art in the Park was a special day. It was fun to see some of the talented artists come to realize their giftedness and share. It is easy to get caught in a "serving" mentality when you are helping the homeless, as if you are the only one giving. On the contrary, I have seen firsthand the difference in those who have "served" on the sidewalk by the school.

One such instance of talent sharing was from Devon, a graffiti artist who had been previously incarcerated due to his art adorning buildings, signs, and bridges. Devon is a truly talented artist; we just wished he might use his gifts for more legal means. Natalie had seen Devon's art and heard his story. She invited him to share his artistic ability with us at Art in the Park.

Gigi bought spray paint just for him and Natalie brought a large bed sheet. Natalie had asked Devon to make a banner for her Bible Project. Initially, Devon suggested he was not worthy of this "honor," but he eventually conceded. A crowd surrounded him as he made quick work of the sheet, layering it with color in beautiful quick passes of the spray can. As the crowd grew, the art began to form and the letters for The Bible Project began to pop. It was an awesome sight to behold and was truly a spectacular piece of art that could rival any paid work. We stood in awe. Natalie was thrilled!

After the piece was complete, and after the meal service was wrapped up, Natalie shared a story with me. It was Devon's story, of his arrests and incarceration and his estrangement from his father who was not proud of his graffiti. Devon's father came with him that day to Art in the Park and watched and marveled, as we all did, at the art Devon had created. His father told him how proud he was of him. It was the first time his father had said that to him, the first time Devon had received affirmation and validation of his giftedness. It was an emotional moment for sure.

The Art in the Park lunch was a unique opportunity, and it attracted some new faces to help with the project. Sarah wasn't a part of our Under the Overpass group. She had never heard of Mission from Mars and wasn't part of our circle of friends or even friends of friends. Sarah happened to work with a friend of Natalie's, Claire. Natalie had stopped by Claire's workplace to drop off one of her colorful Bibles for her. Claire wasn't there, so she ended up talking with Sarah.

"So what do you do with these Bibles?" "Are you a Christian?"

Natalie briefly shared that she serves meals with a homeless mission on the North Shore, and that she passes out her Bibles to those who will accept them.

Sarah was intrigued and later asked her friend Claire more about the group. Claire told her we had an Art in the Park event coming up, and that she should attend. She said, "Count me in." But inside, Sarah was very concerned and tentative.

The day had arrived. Natalie was running a few minutes late to pick up Sarah. Claire was unable to come, and Sarah's nerves and anxieties were building. Natalie called her to ensure she didn't leave the parking lot - she was on her way. They arrived downtown to a bustling scene. Over 100 homeless and likely 20 more volunteers were there, men, women and children among the crowd. Our community has become fond of bringing children down to help serve. They enjoy it so much, and our homeless friends got a little extra smile from seeing the kids. On this day, there were a number of children who were homeless as well. While that is always difficult to see, it was so fun to watch our own children interact with and play with these kids as they would friends from their own neighborhood.

The plan was to have a volunteer work with each homeless individual to create a small canvas or painting of their own. Due to the large numbers that stayed for the art, the volunteers were instead tasked with getting people set-up and organized. They encouraged people to come and paint, draw or create. Sarah, overcoming her own fears, prayed to God, *"God, use me to bless someone. Help me to be your minister of Love. Show me who to talk to and give me back my words that were stolen from me five years ago!"*

Sarah's story is tragic. She had always wanted to help those in need, but her longing began in early 2000 while living in Washington, D.C. during a cold winter. The city was wonderful, except for a "dirty little secret," as she terms it - a quaint little park just two blocks from the White House that was full of homeless people. It was winter and people were sleeping on benches and the ground, with no protection but their clothing. Seeing them broke her heart, and she decided to feed them a meal.

She wondered, "What is their story?"

"How did they get to this point in their lives?"

"Is there no place for them to sleep when it is this cold?"

"When was the last time they ate?"

Sarah didn't have much time to contemplate the questions. Her family was only there for a temporary assignment. She left determined to look further into the homeless situation, but her vigor fizzled as she dealt with some personal issues of her own.

In 1999, her oldest son, Aiden, graduated college and began a several year rebellion against her and God. After many years of heartbreak and hours and hours of a mother's prayer, he began to "straighten up his life and get back on track. He had a heart to help friends who got hooked on drugs, to get clean."

He helped many people, but in January, 2011, he was gone - murdered in his sleep.

"My world went black. We had gone through so much with him and were just coming out the other side...why?"

Sarah had spent the past five years going through the motions, a homeschooling mother with three other children, she kept it together for her children. "They needed me. They needed me to be strong." Sarah and her husband cried in private for their loss. She threw herself into her work, a refuge for the pain - a place for her to escape the memories of her son lost too soon.

"God has carried me the last five years. But I have been useless for Him. I have been broken and wordless. I always felt I needed to 'tell' Aiden's story, but the gift of words God had given me were now silent. My desires to minister for Him were gone. I forced myself to stay in the Word so I could at least stay close to Him. Many days just being held by Him. Over and over asking God,

"What do I do with this? Where do I go from here? No response. I wait and wait and wait!"

Sarah had no ministry at the time, but in the months leading up to her meeting Natalie, she had begun asking where God wanted her, what he wanted her to do.

"How do I serve?" she asked.

In walked Natalie with her infectious energy and obvious spirit.

She asked the Lord, "If this is where you want me, show me you are there."

Sarah prayed about Art and the Park for two months before finally joining us and meeting Matthew.

She was quite nervous at first, taking in everything around her - watching, waiting, and praying.

"Lord, use me," she prayed again.

She began to walk around, admiring the many different types of art.

"What a variety of work. I saw the American Flag, caricatures, abstract painting, and then I saw something that stopped me *still*. It was a painting of a lone cabin in the woods with some pine trees. It was magnificent! It looked so much like a series of paintings my father did many years ago. My father was a wonderful artist. He loved to paint and my house is full of his paintings."

I looked to God and said, "Is this who you want me to talk to?"

"I felt drawn. I commented on his work of art. He made little of it. I asked him, as I sat down beside him, "Where did you learn to paint like that?"

He replied with a very thick accent, "When I was a small boy, about seven, I began to paint."

Sarah and Matthew settled into a long conversation, one that would last over 40 minutes. Matthew was from Poland, a 60- something year old man with white hair and a scruffy beard, quite well groomed for being homeless.

Matthew had been coming to the Sunday meals for about four weeks, and once told me he walks an hour and a half to two hours to come for our meal, staying on the other side of the city.

Beneath the missing front two top teeth and the sadness in his eyes, you can see the remains of a handsome man. He had a gentle, but thickly accented voice.

Sarah began by wanting to know, "What's your story? Why did you come to the States?"

Matthew was reluctant at first, but once the conversation began, a spigot opened up. While Sarah struggled to understand some of his words, she listened and prayed.

Matthew had come to the United States in the late 80's. He worked long hours as a software engineer for a bank in New Jersey for seventeen years. He made $50,000/year plus and was enjoying life in the U.S. He was divorced from his first wife and was ordered to pay child and spousal support. When he later remarried and divorced, the courts again awarded his second wife support. He was very confused by the court's decision.

Then the bottom fell out for Matthew. The bank closed in bankruptcy and he lost everything he had worked for. No job, no pension, no prospects for work. He drove taxis for a while, but now, at his age, he feels very tired.

Abruptly, Matthew turned the tables on Sarah.

He asked, "Do you have children?"

To which she replied as she always did, "Yes, I have four."

Then he said, "I want to know about your oldest. Tell me about him. What happened to him?"

He said it almost knowingly. Sarah swallowed hard and asked for God's help.

Sarah began a short synopsis of what had happened to Aiden. She held her tears, trying to be strong, trying not to cry, not here, not in front of the homeless people with stories sadder than hers. Then Matthew, with the very sad but sparkling blue eyes said, "You are very sad, but he is very happy in heaven." He told her of God's love and told her to pray and ask God for her answers. He said, "God is carrying you, and though you may never know who did this to your son, God knows, and he will take care of it." Sarah had not told him the murder was unsolved. She had also not told him about her dreams. "Tell me about your dreams of Aiden," he said.

Only Sarah's husband Tom knew about her dreams. The realistic and disturbing dreams that leave her with a sense that she has just visited with Aiden. The tears began to flow freely from Sarah. This man, Matthew, who "seemed to know so much," had unleashed a torrent of emotions. He told her the bad dreams were from demons.

"Pray to ask God to remove them. God wants you to smile and be loved. There are angels all around you, helping you. Aiden is with the angels."

Sarah came to Art in the Park to minister to the homeless, but instead she was ministered to. Matthew helped heal Sarah's wounds, to bring back her voice, and allowed her to release all that she was holding deeply inside of her.

As quickly as the conversation began, it ended. Matthew grabbed his two bags and his painting, and walked away, leaving the park.

Sarah had been praying for months for her heart to beat again. It was finally beating and her words had returned!

Many in our group were seeing the fruits of their service, and in my family we were too. My daughters had become regular volunteers and looked forward to their Sunday meals. After our Art in the Park weekend, my daughter's teacher asked all the kids to share what they did that weekend. Alexa told her class how they served the homeless meal and made art with them in the park. She told them how much fun it was and how she gave the picture she painted to one of the homeless men. He was so excited, and he told her that he was going to hang it in his tent. At the conclusion of the share time, the teacher asked the class who exemplified a good citizen.

She then remarked, "Well, I think this is an easy one."

The whole class responded, "Alexa!"

Alexa came home on a cloud that day, feeling so special.

Chapter 9

THE SOUS CHEF

"Do all the good you can, by all means you can, in all the ways you can, in all the places you can, at all the times you can, to all the people you can, as long as you ever can."

John Wesley

When Natalie first began meeting homeless friends, she offered to pray for them. She began decorating and distributing the Bibles to any homeless who wanted them. These highlighted, colorful Bibles have the verses brought to life, and they became something sought after in the homeless community. At one of the early Sunday lunches, Natalie was offering her Bibles to the group of homeless men who were there. When she left, she gave them a business card with her contact information, telling them that if anyone wanted a Bible later to contact her.

Something got lost in translation, and while requests started pouring in, they were not for Bibles. Instead, they were food requests!

"What I wouldn't give for a pork chop."

"What I really miss is macaroni and cheese."

These and many other requests came to her inbox. Some wanted a sleeping bag, and others wanted a tent. Not wanting to turn them away, she mentioned the requests to the group, and the leadership role, the Sous Chef, was born. Lisa and a few others within our Under the Overpass team began to make single portion homemade meals upon request. These meals were made specifically for the individual who had been dreaming about or missing something in particular during their time on the streets. While it certainly ran counter to what John (Natalie's first homeless friend) would have suggested, these Sous Chef meals connected our team in such an incredible way to the people we were serving. The Sous Chefs were by far our most popular volunteers.

We were treating people as if they were family, taking care to provide something they would really like and enjoy. While it was something small, it endeared a number of the homeless to our group and the bonds of friendship continued to grow. On our end, there was a tremendous satisfaction in being able to give someone such a highly prized gift. For many who had been on the streets for a long time, the luxury (or idea) of choosing what to eat was unheard of – certainly not a dish prepared lovingly and solely for them.

The chefs involved received great joy in making these special entrees. The larger missions and shelters were unable to provide personalized meals just because someone missed a favorite food. These small acts of kindness rippled far and wide in our joint homeless/volunteer community.

While many of the missions and shelters attempt to meet basic food needs, the variety is often lacking. A church can more easily provide sandwiches, pizza, or a crock of chili, but it is far more difficult (and expensive) to provide a balanced meal with meats, vegetables, and fruits. Our network of volunteers took great care in our menu planning for the Sunday meal. It was important that we were providing a nutritious and delicious meal. You might ask,

"Why did you consider diversity of the food? Why did you care how the food tasted? If they are starving, won't they eat anything?"

The short answer is yes, they will. If you were starving, you might eat from a dumpster or even off the street. But what happens to your dignity? How do you feel about yourself? In my family, the food is first in every gathering. It is what binds and connects us, as it did with me and my grandmas. We used to cook together, my grandma teaching me how to roll out pasta dough and fill raviolis, or make wedding soup. Many of my fondest memories surround food, either preparing it or eating it.

So what happens when that "family meal" is taken away? What happens when a cold sandwich in a dark room with no friends or family to talk to takes over that experience? Or when we serve in a line with no seating, no opportunity to sit at a table or to break bread with friends? John and I disagree on the importance of the meal. His philosophy was to use the meal to weed out those who don't really need it to survive (by offering bland, lifeless food). In contrast, I want the meal to bring people in, to bring the community together, and for everyone to feel like they belong.

While we were unable to provide tables (other than the two used to serve from) or chairs at the outdoor food service, we had begun to see an evolution over the last few months. Initially, we had a small number of sporadic homeless people hanging in the park. They didn't communicate much with each other and it took a lot for them to engage with us. But now, the community has come alive! We see so much engagement amongst our homeless friends together, as well as with the community at large.

I had a long conversation with one homeless man, Creg, who currently works as a chef in a local restaurant. We talked about the foods our grandparents made and our recipes for sauce. Even though he is employed at a restaurant, he longed to cook for himself and to even teach his skills to others. His current housing does not permit use of the shelter's large kitchen; instead, only crock pots are allowed where he resides. I thought about how much it would affect me if I couldn't cook? Or, if I didn't have the freedom to do what I wanted to do - like relax on my couch (the shelters I have seen are bare bones structures with bunk beds and cement floors, no plush sofas or pleasantries).

I told you that the homeless are often teaching me lessons, and this one was related to the food. The Sous Chef Lisa had dropped off the most delicious Crispy Pork for Tom, a homeless friend. Tom had been waiting eagerly for a couple of weeks for his special delivery, and the day finally arrived. He had requested chops with much enthusiasm, telling the group how much he had missed them during his time living on the streets.

The joy on his face when Tom saw those pork chops was indescribable. He was absolutely ecstatic. Later, when we saw Tom eating the food, we noticed he was sharing them with a woman next to him. While there was enough for Tom, the portion size was not ideal for two people.

Natalie asked him, "Tom, is this your girlfriend?"

He quickly replied, "No, I just met her."

This man who was hungry, who had been dreaming about these pork chops for weeks, shared them with a stranger. Many of the homeless are the most unselfish people I have ever been among. They share their prized pork chops, their food, their tents, sleeping bags, and other meager possessions.

Many who live alone on the streets realize how much they need to rely on one another, offering what little they have selflessly. In our house, we use sharpies to mark our names on leftovers from favorite restaurants so no one else will eat them. Tom could have saved his pork chop for later when he would be hungry, or he could have savored and eaten every last bite. Instead, he shared the meal he had been dreaming about with a woman he didn't know. I was inspired.

On the same cold, dreary day, we had some clothing donations to pass out. Most homeless have only the clothing on their back, so what I witnessed was incredibly humbling. We were distributing pants and had run out again. A man walked over to where we had given them away, and asked if we had any more.

"No, I'm sorry, we just gave away the last pair."

You could tell he was dejected. He needed a new pair of pants as his were incredibly stained and smelled from afar. They were ratty and filled with holes. As I had finished telling him there were no more, a man came over, from out of nowhere. He had received the pair of pants and simply handed them over to the man who asked for them.

"Here, you can have these."

With that, he walked away. No need for thanks or gratitude, he just handed him the pants, no big deal. It was like he was saying, "Don't worry about me, God will provide. Pants aren't that important."

I kept staring at both of them, marveling at what I had just seen. Two men in such obvious need sharing with one another. I had to pause to take it all in. This gesture was so unexpected for me, especially considering my fears that these people would want to take anything that I had!

As we were leaving that day, I found out that Tom, our pork chop recipient, had made plans with the woman he met at our meal. They decided to meet later that night for dinner at the Mission to continue their budding friendship. I left with a huge smile thinking about how in sharing a pork chop, a new friendship was created. A small and simple act of kindness by our Sous Chef had brought significant joy to two people and may have even helped create a new friendship.

The donation of pants allowed one homeless man to sacrifice himself for another.

In my post that week, it made me start to think even more about community and the true meaning of the word.

Jen:

May 1, 2016

Did you know some churches will not welcome the homeless into their midst? Some restaurants will not allow the homeless to stay and eat, even if they are a paying customer?

We served 110 people downtown on a dreary day. Christy has said that one of the camps has a problem with heroin. Another, full of women, has a pregnant woman there. If you went down this weekend, please share your stories!

As the week went on, I implored our group to continue their involvement. The posts in the private Facebook group continued to connect the community.

Jen:

May 4, 2016

Regarding serving for our upcoming weekends - even if the groups are full, if you are an Overpass member, please go! Especially if you have not been before - just please let us know so we know how many to expect! It is so important for us to have as many leaders prepared for fall as possible, so when we come back we can hit the ground running. By going downtown, you are preparing yourself to lead a meal yourself (no contract required!). This group has done such great work and continues to inspire! Here are a few updates:

1. Camp - one of our addicts decided to go into rehab, a huge step! The police and city are frustrated with the camp and drug problems. They are considering a shut down.

2. One of the women who we helped (she was on the street for three months) has been coming back to the Sunday meal for the last couple of weeks. She is now there as a community member - she is now in housing! :)

3. And in big news...HUD (Housing and Urban Development) awarded Allegheny County $3.6 million to deal with homelessness! All of you who want the homeless to have a voice - to advocate for them - this is your time. Let's get that money where it needs to go!

The police were ready to shut down one of the camps. Shutting down the camp would entail taking all of their possessions to a dumpster and leaving them with less than nothing. This was an extremely stressful situation for Christy, who was working with Operation Safety Net to keep the camp open while people could be relocated. It is one thing to close down a camp, but it's another to close it down with nowhere for them to go. Christy and other groups were advocating against the immediate closure, but the public had been complaining about the camp and wanted the homeless out of their backyard.

In the meantime, a new concept was forming to celebrate birthdays on the street. After discovering that many homeless hadn't celebrated their birthdays in years, Gigi decided to do something about it. A team began creating birthday boxes, gifts that could be given in celebration. First time food preparers Petra and her team also shared insights about their experience and what it was like to serve.

Gigi:

May 8, 2016

Another great week! The food looked amazing and there was plenty to eat.

Really quickly before I forget, Derrick's birthday is next Saturday - do we have any of the birthday boxes left?

Also, a request for a large duffel bag and a large drawstring laundry bag if anyone has either of these laying around?

Petra:

May 8, 2016

Hi all. Hope you all have had a great day. Our family has had a great one...thank you for the kind comments about today's meal...it all came together amazingly. I was definitely nervous going in. I found it to be a bit daunting to land on a meal that was able to be made in very large quantities and was transportable. I was hoping that others would participate to make it happen, especially considering that it was Mother's Day, but what if that didn't happen...it turns out that one of the most gratifying parts of the experience was the sense of community of many people just pitching, in some cases even small pieces of the need list, to make the entire experience work.

And then today, the atmosphere was so kind and peaceful. Once we and others with the food arrived, it all just smoothly fell into place. There were more than enough volunteer helpers but everyone just found some role to play, serving, chatting, wrapping food, etc. The kids were awesome, serving food and then going around to offer the last yogurts and fruit. My children were a little nervous going in but both volunteered that it was a great experience and they would like to do it again.

Everyone we served was grateful. I can't stop thinking about one woman, she was in a wheelchair. We helped her to get a small to-go bag together as we were wrapping up and she mentioned that she had two grandchildren that were in an apartment but they did not have food, but she did not want to be greedy.... We got some to-go packages together for her and she was so grateful.

There was an audible groan from the group when it was mentioned that the last meal for now would probably be at the end of May. The idea of at least once a month or on certain weeks of the summer sounds like a good one. Some of the volunteers that were there today offered that they would like to host or continue to help. Thanks to all that helped me/my family and neighbors this weekend. It was great to meet some of you in person vs. just through this online group. Jen, thanks for holding my hand! And thank you for this opportunity.

Natalie: *Thank you Petra!! I think you are such a great mentor for others that are nervous out of their mind thinking about pulling this off. I was the exact same way!!!! But the joy of the fellowship and connecting with so many new people (with and without homes) is hard to describe! Thanks again for taking the leap!!!*

Laura: *Beautiful day today! The sun was shining and it brought out a big crowd. We served about 65 people. Everyone loved the food and they LOVED the raffles. Let's keep that going! (The group had begun raffling a couple $5 gift cards at lunch. We gave a raffle ticket to everyone that went through the line to get a more accurate head count. These were of course donated by a generous volunteer.)*

Shout out to Petra and her family and team! The food was delish and our friends loved it. Ham is a great meal. It's easy and they can make sandwiches or eat it warm.

The flowers for the women were a beautiful touch. They really loved them. I saw one woman who was beaming. She looked beautiful and loved having some pretty flowers. <u>Natalie,</u> Great idea!! (Another special item that day - flowers were given to all the women in attendance for Mother's Day. A little, special something to show we cared.)

Everyone I spoke with today blessed me for being there and taking the time to do this for them. And all of them wished us a Happy Mother's Day. It was heartwarming.

They were SO SO grateful for our meal today and were sad that we will be ending service soon for summer break. That weighed heavy on my heart--is anyone out there willing to continue in some capacity? I know I would be happy to do a couple of weeks as long as I know in advance. Maybe we can do it every other week for the summer? Or once a month? If we tell them it will be the first Sunday of each month (June/July/August) they'll know to come down??? Just thinking out loud.

I promised a few men some shoes. I wish I asked their names - Christy knows them. Chris I think? And someone named Slick...I don't know if I'll be down next week but will get them to someone. If anyone has size 10-11 (and half sizes) of men's shoes from husbands, feel free to post and I'll pick them up. I'm sure we can always use them. Happy Mother's Day everyone!

Sunday Lunch - Mother's Day

The replies began to pour in positively. People didn't want the lunches to end, and they were willing to step up to make it happen.

> **_Laura:_** _OK, let's do this ladies! We might have a skeleton crew but I think we can do at least once a month. I'll post another thread and get a little more specific._

> **_Gigi:_** _As long as I'm in town, I can pitch in!_

> **_Laura:_**

> _May 13, 2016_

> _Hi All--_
> _I met with Jen and Christy this week and we chatted about summer._

> _We were in agreement that serving once a month would be a HUGE help to our friends. Sure, we'd love to do more but we cannot burn out. We all have a gazillion things on our plate so I think once a month would be a nice compromise. Let's start there and if someone has it in their heart to take an extra Sunday, let me know._

We decided to do the LAST Sunday of each month to make it easy on our friends. We will also put a note on the Mission door. Doing the last Sundays of each month allows us to avoid holiday weekends when many of us will be away.

Christy has a few groups for June so I told her we'd take care of July, August and September. The dates are listed below. Please let me know if you would like to be a meal host AND/OR if you can help serve.

With Laura and Gigi's new leadership, Christy's resources, and some Overpass members committing to additional dates, the meals would continue through the summer!

Jen:

May 22, 2016

If you haven't yet seen the video Christy posted on MFM site - go there and share it. A great man on the scene for what is happening on Sunday (in case you've never been)!

So, the crowds keep growing! We served around 100 people at the site today, plus camps! I can't believe this is true, but I have it on good authority that Kelly's amazing troop brought 100 lbs of ground meat - and that it was all gone! They also brought some new favorites - frozen "gogurts" and juice, were gone quickly. They also loved the flavored waters and LOVED the taco and ice cream bars. I think one of the coolest things about this group is that there is no question we would eat this food and/or serve it to our own families!

Shout outs to Alaina, Allison, Gigi, Lisa and all the other regulars and new faces!

A couple stories - as I am told some of you like my rambles - got to see Creg again today. He starts school tomorrow and is very excited! He's been working with LIVING Ministries to help them cook meals on days they don't have anyone to donate them. As you know, Creg is one of our friends and he is also a talented chef. Love to hear when one of our own is able to give of their talents! Creg would like to do a cooking class and I would like to make it happen for him. If you have ideas, message me. And be on the lookout for more info as we figure something out!

Lots of young kiddos and families today - and many of those kids took an extra meal for tonight. I'm glad they will have food and that my kids got to play with them at the park and bring them some joy!

Yvonne was so excited to tell me she signed a lease and will be getting out from under the bridge soon! I am thrilled for her, and Mark, who was also there beaming with excitement! (Mark was the recipient of the portable shelter.)

I love to tell the good stories, but I am also compelled to share the others. In talking with Tim today, he seemed like mentally he wasn't all there. He was almost threatening to one of our Overpass members that was not there this week (I have contacted this person directly). I redirected the conversation and walked away, but we have to be mindful of this in our midst. It is the hardest part of this for me, and I know many of you share my concerns. But I am hopeful that our calm will help in processing those emotions in some way, but please be always aware!

Final notes - next week is the big party date! I know many of you are making food to either bring or send down. If you plan to go, can you please let _Allison_ and _Lisa_ know so they can send their food with you?

This is a special place, this Overpass community, and I am so glad to have all of you here with us. Thank you so much for everything you have done this spring. Who knew we could accomplish so much, feed so many people, and be directly involved in getting people relocated to shelter in small ways!

Chapter 10

NATALIE'S CHURCH

"But seek first the kingdom (of God) and his righteousness, and all these things shall be given you besides."

Matthew 6:33

Not long after the Art in the Park event, Natalie was asked to speak at her church about the Bible Project. I had heard bits and pieces of the story, but didn't really know all the details. I thought it would be a good opportunity to hear what she had to say and also support a friend. Driving up to the church building, I could already see some differences from churches I had previously visited. There were parking lot attendants, and I immediately felt like I was going to an event at a stadium rather than a church. I met Natalie and two of her three small children outside, and I was again reminded just how hard it is for people with kids to volunteer.

With a child on one arm and the others being dragged along with all manner of bags and paraphernalia, we walked into the church. I jokingly remarked how lucky she was that I was there, fully expecting her toddlers to sit on my lap and crawl all over me during the service. I prepared to hear less of the story (while I helped with her children), but was glad I came to lend a hand.

To my surprise, the children were instead taken to beautiful childcare areas that looked like they were from a Dr. Seuss cartoon. Kids delivered, we moved on to the main church area.

Natalie was called to prepare with the pastor, and I took our seats in the second row of the church. This wide-open space with office building style chairs, expansive ceilings, jumbotron style projection screens, and full band set-up, was in stark contrast to the more traditional churches I have visited. Gone was the altar dressed in cloth. In its place was a fully enclosed drum kit, I assume for sound muffling. There were microphones and speakers and bar stool style chairs. As I sat alone in my chair waiting for the service to start, I started to feel a bit out of place.

When Natalie rejoined me, Christy also arrived to support Natalie in the sharing of her story.

The lights dimmed and a woman who could be on some sort of musical tour began to sing. It was loud! People were clapping and we were being asked to sing along. I looked down at the small pamphlet of paper on my chair, searching for the words, when Christy directed me to the screens in front of me and to both sides. The lyrics floated on-screen as if it were karaoke. It was like I was onstage, sitting in the second row, reading lyrics to songs I had never heard, to tempos I have never heard in church.

When the band finished, the pastor called onto the stage a couple people from the audience to join him. They shared their own stories - stories of the Kingdom Projects. I had mentioned these projects earlier as being the impetus for the Bible Project and portable shelter creation, but at the time had no idea what they were talking about.

As the speakers continued, I wondered, where were the readings? Where was the Gospel? The service was not arranged in a way that was familiar to me. But, I listened intently. The first person called to the floor was actually the initial church pastor, who now holds some sort of honorary helping role. He explained the vision of the church and how it related to service. Having recently been inspired to participate in the homeless mission, I could see the connection he was drawing between church and community.

The next speakers became a bit of a blur, and then Natalie arrived onstage. She sat on a bar stool and was given a microphone. She was illuminated with stage lighting and her smile concealed her nerves...at least for a short while. When she began to talk, she began to explain how nervous she was, that this was not something in her comfort zone.

"I think I'm going to throw up," actually left her lips!

We smiled encouragingly from the audience, so close but far away.

The pastor settled in with some "softball" questions, an interview type session.

"How did you get started with this 'Bible Project' and "What made you want to do this?"

All eyes turned to Natalie, who began her story. Her story of reading about the homeless and of her vacation to Miami, where she was struck by both the poverty and riches she was seeing all around her. On one side were elaborate hotels, on the other, the darkness of the streets.

She wanted to do something, but didn't want to give money that might be used for drugs. She decided to pass out her leftover food from dinner, and went home determined to think things through.

Once back at home, Natalie decided to search for ways to help the homeless in Pittsburgh, and she stumbled upon Christy's group, Mission from Mars, on Facebook. Christy had created the group in November, 2016 to sponsor a donation drive for the Mars Home for Youth, a residence for children who have experienced trauma. The drive was initiated after Christy got word that these children were asking for towels and sheets for Christmas wish list items.

Seeing a need in the homeless community in December, Christy and her sons decided to bring leftover food from hotels to people on the streets as part of an Eagle Scout project. She immediately connected with the people living in the park and began to visit weekly. She and her friend Bonnie would bring a crock pot of soup or something small to share and would engage in conversations. Christy began posting these stories on her Mission from Mars Facebook page to raise awareness.

Natalie was now calm as she fluently continued her story. As she searched for something to do locally, one particular post caught her eye.

"Wanted: Port a Potty for the Homeless." That wasn't the exact title, but it did make Natalie think about something she had never thought about; the bathroom needs of the homeless.

The actual posting from Christy and Mission from Mars was quite poetic in a very raw way. Two days after Christmas, this post ignited a storm of likes, shares, and action. In all, it reached almost 84,000 people.

Mission from Mars

Christy:

December 27, 2015

> *No words for today. 12 men live here on the South Side of Pittsburgh. We went into their home under the bridge and found out their needs. Young and old live here. They were all wonderful, making a lot of jokes for being embarrassed of their home. Normal*

people down on their luck, or yes, addicted. I told them no judgments from us. They need shovels, thermal underwear, firewood, hand sanitizer, toilet paper, paper products, camping supplies, pots and pans. And yes a Port a John! I see 2-3 everywhere around the city not being used and these guys have none! Loved, loved, the thermal emergency blankets!! Putting them on top of their tents!! And yes "Honey" the Chihuahua lives here and loves bologna sandwiches and hates dog food. lol. Biggest Chihuahua I ever saw. lol. Who can make something happen? Who has old camping stuff to get rid of? Who knows someone to get these guys wood delivered? One said shovels so they can make money over winter and make their environment safe for walking. Who can help, I am willing to do porch pick-ups and deliver with the MFM team. Who has ideas?

Homeless living area

The post sparked Natalie to do something about what had been bothering her. It inspired her to research a solution. The problem: homeless bathroom needs under the overpass.

Natalie once told me privately about a disabled veteran living in the camp that the potty was eventually placed in. He was unable to climb over the embankment to relieve himself. Feces, food, and people all in the same place seem to be an ideal recipe for rats, and, I would also think infectious disease!

Natalie searched and eventually came upon a camping toilet, which she purchased for the encampment area. She was not yet ready to venture under the bridge, but she did begin meeting Christy in a park in the North Side of Pittsburgh. They began to meet new people, all homeless, and would bring some food down with them.

Friendships developed, particularly between Jose, a homeless man, and Natalie's husband Rob. They share a love of all things sports, and Rob began to bring sports magazines or the newspaper. They could both talk sports at length. If you saw Jose in the dead of winter, you would wonder if he was part bear. He's tall, with a thick gray, white and black, long beard, and his dark brown jacket covers a large frame. This bulk could also be due to the sheer number of layers he is wearing, I estimate at least ten. He ties his hoodie tightly around his face, so all you can see is a nose, a bit of two large, brown eyes, and part of his scruffy beard.

If you passed him on the street, he might just blend into the sidewalk, averting most people. His posture and air are very unassuming, in an off-putting kind of way. What you might notice were the two shopping carts he lugs with him everywhere he goes, his only earthly possessions anchored to them in blue plastic shopping bags - full carts, remnants of a life on the street. *Jose has been on the street for over 25 years*, an eternity for a man living in the elements, with no protection from the cold, no warmth, no bed. Jose sleeps in a small, rickety, folding chair under a bridge. He's very private, but not anti-social.

After hearing Natalie's testimony to her church about the Kingdom Projects, it made me really see the difference one person or action can have. If Christy had never brought food for the first time, if the Pastor hadn't created or promoted the Kingdom Project, if Natalie hadn't been inspired by her trip to Miami, none of us would be meeting the people we were meeting, and this community would have never developed. It seems no coincidence that all of these things coincided with the things happening in my own life. We could sense an invisible hand guiding us.

After meeting the homeless for the first time, Natalie later found a quote that perfectly articulated her feelings.

> *"The world is not yours to change. None of us is big enough, influential enough, or powerful enough to end any one of the world's major issues. The only person powerful enough to eradicate poverty... is Jesus."*

> - Michael Yankoski, *Under the Overpass*

The issues are just too great, too large for any person to comprehend, fathom, or begin to fix.

Shortly after her talk at church, Natalie posted this to her new Bible Project Facebook page:

The Bible Project:

April 21

A few months ago, the Bible Project was started. Have you ever seen a Bible that has been loved? I saw my 91 year old grandmother's Bible and it was a beautiful testament of His love for us. Imagine –

to love and pray over a Bible - then give it away to those that may feel unlovable. What a gift that would be. That is what we are doing with The Bible Project. We are loving and praying over 4x6 Bibles through highlighting, writing notes, and drawing, to be shared as an encouraging gift.

After spending time with the homeless in Pittsburgh, I found we are more the same than we are different. We are all searching, fighting to stay free, weary and maybe we are reaching a point where we just want to shut down. But my friends under the bridge taught me God is working in every moment of our life for the life He designed. With our trust in Him, He promises us we have a purpose.

These last few months, we have been going through a journey. Scroll till your heart content for more, but here is where we have been....

- His Word is a gift.
- We were bought. Redeemed. By the blood of Christ.
- We prayed. About loneliness, strength, rest for the weary, courage, anxiety and worry.
- Through the mission "to transform lives to find hope in God's Word and while doing this, be transformed. God's Word refreshes the soul, gives wisdom, gives joy to the heart, enlightens the eyes and endures forever." I asked you all to spend the month of April in Prayer.
- So we prayed to pray
- To pray and remember we are the child of the King!
- To pray against being too busy to be in His word
- To Be Inspired and Be Thankful for the beautiful people around us sharing their talents and time for His glory.
- And to surrender.

Thank you for joining in this great adventure of loving the Word of God.

During this past month of prayer, I committed to pray for others. I joined a group where women poured out their prayer requests and I got down on my knees to pray.

And so began Natalie's journey, one of helping the homeless, but really of meeting people and treating them as people - seeing them as God sees them, with compassion and grace, love and respect. Have you ever really thought about what would be missing in your life if no one saw you in that way?

If people walking down the street yelled at you to "Get a job you bum," or worse, how would you feel? Would you be proud and boastful, arrogant and tall?

In the months that have passed since I began to know Natalie and Christy, we have had many conversations about how the homeless on the street really "feel." How so many of their hearts are empty, how they feel "unlovable."

They might say to you, "I am Broken. Hopeless, Bad, Lost, Bitter and Insecure. I'm Dead Inside. I am Suffering, Alone and Tired. I am a Loser. I'm Helpless. I have No Life and NO PURPOSE."

Their souls are defeated and weary. They can't foresee an end to their struggles, their misery. It's so difficult to dwell on that suffering, their suffering - so many people going through such tremendous hardships. Thinking back to when I was in the hospital, I find it hard to compare my suffering to theirs - the cumulative effect of being cold, alone, helpless, and hungry. Their pain so much worse, simply because of the comforts that surrounded me. I had many friends and family members praying for me, people visiting me, nurses and doctors caring for me; inside shelter, with all the luxuries we take for granted every day.

As I contemplate what it would be like to be sick and homeless, with illnesses from epilepsy to incontinence, surviving those hardships on the street would be an almost insurmountable suffering. And yet they survive. And even thrive. And some even find complete conversions and turnarounds in their lives.

I wrote the following for the Mission from Mars website, based on information we gathered about the friends we were meeting.

"What's it Really Like to be Homeless?"

Imagine it's 20 degrees outside. It's cold. I may or may not have shoes or a coat, a hat, or gloves. I may have a tent or live under an overpass. I may have found an alley that has a small amount of shelter, or I may sleep in a port a potty or dumpster. If it rains, I have no way to dry my belongings. They may get moldy. If I have a blanket, it may freeze solid.

I may not have eaten today, or yesterday, or even the day before.

I may work. If I do, there are challenges. How do I get clean? The clothes I have on are the only clothes I have. Anything I walk away from or leave will be stolen from me. I'm robbed regularly. I can only keep what I can carry, often in a small backpack if I have one.

I typically walk to work, often for miles and carrying all of my belongings. My shoes may have holes and my feet may hurt. I may be cold, smell, need a shave, or haircut. I walk long distances to get washed up, or I might even use the river.

I may have been in jail. I may owe money for child support. I may be saving up to have a place of my own. I may have a problem with addiction.

Rats are a huge problem. I have to be careful where I eat and go to the bathroom to keep them away. Rats may have eaten through my clothes, cans of food, and even my cooler if I am lucky enough to have one.

I may be partially blind or disabled. I may be a parent, a grandparent, a veteran, a relative, a friend, or even a child. I may have been raped, possibly even in a shelter. I may be on the streets waiting for space to open up in a shelter. I may be newly homeless or I may have been living on the street for a year or more. I may be saving money for rent, or a security deposit, or a bus ticket to see my child.

I may have been robbed and no longer have identification or a driver's license. This makes it difficult to open a bank account, get a job, cash a check, or find a place to live.

I may lose faith that people care about me. I may have been spit on.

I am often embarrassed of my circumstances and may not want to ask for help.

I may be sick. I may be dying. **I am most certainly the strongest person you will ever meet!**

How do these people, these absolutely broken people, people who the world has discarded and cast off as lepers, how do they exhibit more strength than others?

They are strong by necessity on the street, pushing through and enduring. But in all their brokenness, I have found that many have incredible spirit. They believe so much in God, even though they suffer so much. They quote scripture in ways I never expected. I am amazed by their ability to get up and live another day.

Natalie asked us why we serve the homeless, on a post it note, her favorite mode of communication. I struggled to answer her. I feel like it's a very multi-pronged answer, part selfish, part spiritually directed and part just feel good. For me, the feel good doesn't happen beforehand; thinking about helping doesn't really do it for me. It's the actual helping, the actual hands on experience and the response to that helping, the feedback that comes from doing something for others. It is like a rush in a way, an addiction or any other high. I think you can truly get "drunk" on the high of helping others. I think Christy is one of those people. She needs the rush that helping brings - the feeling of fulfillment knowing you have done something for others. It fills a place inside you and pushes you to do more.

I don't know if I am wired exactly the same way. I have to push myself into these circumstances, push myself out of my comfort zone. Even after serving the homeless for months, I don't yearn to do it again. I recognize the good, yet I don't really want to go. I want to stay in my comfortable home and forget these problems exist.

But there is a draw for me. A spirit within me that tells me I should do more. I can do more. I hear the messages at church and I know they are intended for me - that I should give more of myself, but it is not easy for me. It's easy for me to make excuses and say I am too busy. It would be easy for me to stop seeing them. If I didn't see them, I wouldn't have to feel their pain that is so real for me. I experience it down into the fiber of my being. Their hurt, their suffering - I feel it so deeply that I have to turn away. I have to get away from it. My body is pushing me away and drawing me closer to them, to their pain, all at the same time.

Recently, friends I have known for a long time have been telling me how proud of me they are. What a change they see in me. How I seem different. It is hard to understand, but I feel different. I feel changed by them, by the homeless I have met - changed by their pain and their suffering. The magnitude of their highs and lows has intensified my own highs and my lows. I cheer in their successes and I feel that rush, that feeling of good. But I also feel that darkness when they overdose on heroin, and I recognize there is nothing I can do for them.

There are so many problems and they run so deep. How can anyone really help? How can anyone solve their problems? It is such a great burden to know of the pain and problems, but to feel powerless to help. I wanted to fix every problem, but I couldn't. Only God could fix them. Only God could fix this. But offering that up is not easy. Putting it in God's hands is not easy. It is a struggle, an intense struggle, where I feel I need to use my talents and gifts, but all my gifts and talents are inadequate. It is humbling and difficult. As Natalie likes to remind me, there are times we have to be still. Be still and listen. Be still and know that only He is God.

Chapter 11

YVONNE

"Home is the nicest word there is."

Laura Ingalls Wilder

I received a note that said Mark, the recipient of the first portable homeless structure, or igloo, would be moving into an apartment. Upon hearing the news, the excitement and enthusiasm in the Overpass group increased to yet unseen levels. Mark is a veteran and has the warmest personality. He has short, medium brown hair, and dark brown skin. He takes care of himself and has always appeared pretty clean and well groomed. Mark is disabled, and we were so glad to see him moving to a new place. His disability made the unbearable winter homeless existence even harder, due to the difficulties of navigating the camp and the above-mentioned bathroom situations.

It was quickly apparent that we wanted to do something for him, but what? Tammy, who first joined us downtown during Art in the Park, offered to collect a few housewarming items. While we had previously collected for camps, this would be our first true Welcome Wagon for someone in a home!

Tammy:

May 18, 2016

I've been in touch with Christy, and she has confirmed that our friend, Mark, has indeed secured a home!! I thought it would be nice to get some housewarming items together for him from this team. Christy is able to get a bed, and he will be receiving some larger furniture. He has food stamps so should be able to take care of his own food needs. Let's try to get some of the following items for him (used and in good shape are perfect!). I will collect them and then we can either get a small group together to take them down to him, or Christy and Bonnie can take them down. If you can get any of these items, please comment! You can drop them off at my house or I can meet you somewhere.

-sheets (full/double)
-comforter (full/double)
-plates and bowls
-cups
-utensils
-lamps
-small furniture items such as TV trays, small tables, etc
-towels/washcloths
-cleaning supplies/sponges/dish soap
-kitchen towels
-small kitchen garbage can
-kitchen garbage bags
-shower curtain and liner
-bathroom garbage can
-laundry basket
-napkins/paper towels/paper towel holder
-pots and pans
-serving utensils
-glass bowls
-measuring cups/spoons
-small radio/tv

What's it like collecting for someone who is homeless and moving into a place? It's very different than a traditional Welcome Wagon. They have nothing: no bed, no sheets, no furniture, no food, no dishes, glassware, silverware...you name it, they don't have it. They have what they had with them under the bridge, which typically includes the clothes on their back, maybe a grocery bag of belongings, and if they are blessed, a tent. That's it! This makes unpacking go very quickly.

Tammy got us organized and made a list of what was needed, and the Overpass group responded in full force. A big part of the excitement was the fact that even though we hoped people would get into homes, we didn't know if anyone would. While Christy had the joy of seeing two people get into a new place, the rest of us had not experienced it. As we busily collected house wares, something incredible happened. We found out that another one of our homeless, Yvonne, was signing a lease and getting out too, soon! We doubled our efforts to ensure we would have supplies for not one, but two of our friends!

At the same time, Natalie tried to prepare our volunteers, so they were better equipped to lead meals if we were absent on a Sunday.

Natalie:

May 21, 2016

YOU are invited to a concierge party.

Summer is around the corner and I'm itching for a party! I am planning to host a fire pit party for anyone who is willing to serve at least once this fall as a 'concierge.' haha. Yes, bribing you with a party. I know Tammy is coming to my party. Who else wants in??

A Concierge is the go to person for a 'newbie' who wants to make a meal for a Sunday. You've made or hosted a meal before and you've been downtown to serve. You don't have to make the meal, but you are the go to person for questions, for 'safety,' directing them to important info on the website. You meet them downtown on Sunday or arrange for someone to meet them. You help make sure there is a mix of newbies and experienced volunteers.

Who's in so I can plan a party...

Tammy:

May 22, 2016

Happy Sunday, friends! Please see below for housewarming items I have already received and items that have been committed. Note that we now have TWO homeless friends currently getting into housing - Mark and Yvonne - so the more items we can collect, the better! I will divide whatever items we gather into two housewarming sets. If you haven't already, please try to get me any items you would like to contribute by Friday, May 27th. I'm happy to meet you wherever to pick up your donations!! Stay tuned on delivery of the items--I really would like to get a small group to go deliver them personally to Mark and Yvonne once they are in their apartments...maybe bring a small meal, too! Thanks all!

I HAVE ALREADY RECEIVED: 4 plates, 4 bowls, 4 sets silverware, 4 glasses, 4 mugs, 4 placemats, a pizza pan, pizza cutter, one spatula, 2 pieces Tupperware, 1 set cleaning supplies (bucket, general cleaners and soaps, dish brush, dustpan and brush, laundry detergent, sponges), 1 blanket, 1 full size comforter

Natalie:

May 24, 2016

All - I'm just so proud of all of you. You all amaze me with your generosity and drive and passion to want to change things. I think all of you are part of a huge movement and all we need is a desire to make something happen.

I'm thankful that so many leaders are stepping up. The power that we have here - if you want to lead, you can. You are generous and authentic and you are leading change in our community.

What is beautiful is that there is no president here, no hierarchy, no organization (I know, Laura wants to get this place organized), but it's so many people - not from a church, not from a certain belief, not from similar hobbies or interests. We are a band of people, a tribe that believes in loving our neighbors. And that makes me happy.

So thanks for making me happy. Thanks for loving each other and loving our community. Thank you for stepping up and jumping in, helping others to jump in and throwing fears out the door.

You all know who you are but thank you for jumping in with your hearts (not your ever-loving mind) to try to extend the community meals through the summer, thanks for organizing groups to get together to walk, talk, gather backpacks. Thanks for organizing 'Welcome Wagon' packages as we get excited for friends to find a home. And just thank you. Thank you for being remarkable and not worry about the rest, the criticism, the fears.

The criticisms Natalie referenced are now common for me, but this was one of the first times people in our group had been confronted for "publicity seeking." While we knew why we were helping and felt our motives were pure, we received criticism.

This saddened many of us and kept more than a few from posting publicly or telling people about what we were doing. The reality was that if we failed to share with the masses, the mission could not be sustained.

If we fail to share our stories, we fail to inspire others. We selfishly keep it to ourselves, not allowing others to follow. Interestingly enough, according to PTOToday.com, one of the prime reasons people don't volunteer is that they feel they somehow don't measure up.

By sharing stories with friends and them seeing us as peers and equals, it made it easier for other people to get involved.

It will be easy for people to criticize me in writing this book, asking the question, "Aren't you hypocritical living in a nice house and taking vacations while you are aware of such need around you?" My answer to this, like many surrounding the homeless, "It's complicated."

Having resources has allowed me and others to do for those in need. But of course, we can always do more. I choose to subscribe to the notion that it's better to do something than nothing. I have chosen to share our stories in an attempt to inspire others to give even a little bit of themselves, a small amount of their time and resources, because if everyone did just a little, I believe the world would be a better place.

But even criticism could not contain our exuberance. In a hasty note, we were told that Yvonne would be moving in the next day! She received notice from the Homeless Assistance program that she would be placed in an apartment after a very long year and a half living outdoors!

Tammy mobilized a small team, including myself, to help distribute the items we collected. I couldn't sleep that night. I told myself it was because my room was hot, but I know it was because I was so looking forward to seeing Yvonne in a different surrounding. To see her not as a homeless person, but as a friend that had moved into a new place. There were so many possibilities for her, and I wanted to see her realize this dream.

What else could I give her?

What might she find useful?

Does she like to read or do crossword puzzles?

Does she have any furniture at all?

What will the place be like?

Where is it located?

Will it be safe?

How will she afford it?

My mind swirled in 100 directions, and I couldn't stop thinking. I couldn't shut off. Thinking about what her first shower would be like (turns out it was a long bubble bath) or what her first meal that she cooks for herself would be (pasta) kept me up. Finally, morning came! I awoke with a fire and vigor. My step was lighter, my smile bigger, and I couldn't wait to get started on my day!

First stop, my office at the church (yep, I need to back up a step here- I now work at a church!).

In a twist of crazy "coincidences," the person who was supposed to take the position of Outreach Coordinator at my church had decided not to start after all. When I literally bumped into my priest in the stairwell at my son's First Holy Communion, I happened to ask about her. He had previously told me to connect with the new hire and share what we were doing with Mission from Mars, that he wanted the parish to get involved. He said they were currently looking for someone, and in an off-hand way, he suggested I send in my resume. I interviewed just a couple days later.

I wasn't looking for a job and had been happy with the contract work I had been doing. I had no idea what the position entailed, other than knowing that the prior Coordinator had given supplies to my Faith Formation class.

During the interview, Father led us in prayer which brought me back to the fact that this was a church and not a typical employer.

We talked about Christy and Mission from Mars and my new homeless friends. And I explained to them how I had been considering working with Mission from Mars on a more full-time basis, helping to take the organization to non-profit level.

Something was holding me back from committing to Mission from Mars in that way. The timing was off, and my vision was somehow different or maybe more global.

In discussing the opportunity before my interview, my husband Joe said to me, "All the things you want to do can be done through the church."

In my interview, when I told them what he said, things clicked for me. It was as though God had given me Mission from Mars to get to this place, to involve a bigger community. To my extreme surprise, I was offered the position hours after my interview, accepted, and that brings us back to the present.

There were two old lamps sitting in my office from my predecessor, and I had received permission to share them with my friends. So, I stopped at work to pick up lamps to give to Tammy for our two homeless friends who were getting into apartments. When I walked in the building, everyone around me could sense just how much energy I had. While in the office, it dawned on me that I had more to give! I had blessing bags that were made by Faith Formation children. They were filled with shampoos, soaps, washcloths, blankets, crossword puzzles, and even an iTunes gift card! I felt like I had hit the lottery, that I could share these riches with my friends!

Rumor had it that the church also kept some supplies to give to someone who might show up at the door in need, so I asked if I could take those as well. Much to my surprise, I was given two food store gift cards totaling $50! One of the staff suggested I could also take food, which was in the food pantry collection box.

I rushed to the box, thinking it would be empty since I had met with the Food Collection ministry just the day before and they had emptied it...but it was full once again! Cans of vegetables, boxes of pasta, rice, jars of fruit. I eagerly grabbed all that I could carry and filled my SUV, which was now overflowing with gifts for our friends. And I had a final thought - we are a church, we should have a cross that we could deliver with this bounty. So, I went in search of a cross, and found two beautiful crosses that were in a bin of unused and ready-to-be-discarded Faith Formation items. Along with them were two tiny nativity scenes. These were absolutely perfect! With the car finally loaded, I headed off to Tammy's house to help deliver the goods.

When I arrived in the driveway, Gigi from our Overpass group was unloading her trunk into Tammy's already full garage. It was incredible to see all of the items collected in such a short period of time, less than one week to outfit two apartments! I unloaded my car, and we divided the items so each would receive an end table, food, sheets, and kitchen supplies. When we realized Yvonne would have no can opener, Tammy quickly texted Alaina, who was going to be delivering with us, and asked her to stop for one. Without hesitation, Alaina said, "Of course."

The selflessness I have seen in this group of people is the perfect definition of 'love thy neighbor.' This special place, this collection of friends of friends who want to do something...be something better, has been so inspiring.

When I look back at the women who went on that Welcome Wagon with us, Tammy, Gigi, and Alaina, they were all relative strangers to me. I met each and every one of them through the Under the Overpass group, but we talked, joked, and laughed together like old friends. There was an immediate, special bond that had formed between us.

As I stood in the driveway, Christy pulled up in her packed minivan. Christy was another person who I had begun spending a lot of time with, and I developed a deep respect for her passion and heart. We were together on this quest, and we were learning a lot from her experiences and encounters.

Christy arrived with the seats folded down to accommodate a full mattress in the back of the van. There were bags of items in the front seat and everyone was smiling ear to ear.

Believing that what we were witnessing could only happen but a few times in our lifetimes, we wanted to savor it. I don't know what the odds or chances are of going from living on the streets to living in an apartment, completely independently, but they can't be great. We were witnessing a miracle and it made us tear up.

After Alaina arrived with the new can opener and a car full of cereals and extra supplies, we caravanned to Yvonne's. The cars were so full that we had to take two vans and one large SUV. I couldn't believe it was happening, but I was also afraid. I was afraid of where we were going and what we were going to encounter - a fear of the unknown. Would Yvonne be excited to see us? Would she appreciate the items we collected? Would we be safe? Will she be safe? As you can see, bravery was not an attribute I had yet discovered.

At that moment, a peace descended upon me, and I heard the words I had read the day before, "Do not be afraid." That prior day, I had been following along in my Facebook Bible study with Natalie, and this is the section she had sent to me:

Luke 2:1-21- NIV

> *The Birth of Jesus*
> *And there were shepherds living out in the fields nearby, keeping watch over their flocks at night. An angel of the Lord appeared to them, and the glory of the Lord shone around them, and they were terrified. But the angel said to them, "__Do not be afraid.__ I bring you good news that will cause great joy for all the people. Today in the town of David a Savior has been born to you; he is the Messiah, the Lord. This will be a sign to you: You will find a baby wrapped in cloths and lying in a manger."*
>
> *Suddenly a great company of the heavenly host appeared with the angel, praising God and saying,*
>
> *"Glory to God in the highest heaven,*
> *and on earth peace to those on whom his favor rests."*

I sent this reply to Natalie on the same day:

Jen:

> *Have you ever noticed that when angels appear they almost always tell the people...do not be afraid?*

Looking at this just one day later, I am amazed that those were the exact words I heard in my head in the car ride down with Tammy.

The *do not be afraid* comment couldn't have come at a better time, as Tammy and I were extremely anxious. We had been assessing our surroundings, and the neighborhood did not appear safe at all. There were lots of young men milling about, and our minivans really stood out. We had no protection - no gun, no pepper spray, no mace. In hindsight, we could have planned better for our surroundings.

I relayed the voice in my head to Tammy in the car and as we began to relax, we saw a police car. We felt some protection in knowing we were doing something good, but we took that police car as a sign we would be OK. It was only a half block away and it was the affirmation we needed to keep going. I have never been so grateful to see a police car.

Feeling calm and excited once again, we arrived at Yvonne's. She looked good was my first thought - cleaner, happier, and her spirit seemed lighter. While she wasn't smiling, she was joking and gave Christy and then the rest of us a hug. She thanked us for coming, and in an almost businesslike way, directed us to where we could park and bring the items.

The apartment had been somewhat updated inside, but I feared for Yvonne in this neighborhood. Outside the door to the apartment was a very real reminder of what type of neighborhood we were in. There was a large, stained mattress. We were told to avoid this mattress as it was filled with bed bugs. As you can imagine, we were quite careful in unloading and bringing items into the residence.

Having brought my young daughter and Tammy's young son, we were careful to keep a close eye on them while unpacking. Once the kids settled into an unpacking role in the apartment, we began to form an assembly line bringing items from the cars to the house. It struck me that I didn't see Yvonne helping, that she was simply standing in the apartment.

After taking a load inside with Tammy and delivering an end table to Yvonne's new room, she began to sob in a long embrace with Tammy. She was so overwhelmed. Paralyzed by it. She saw all of these things, things that were hers, things she said she didn't need. When you have lived for so long with almost nothing, the "stuff" we delivered, while not furniture or anything that I would have considered abundant, seemed too much for her. You could see an inner reflection and it was easy to recognize that she was thinking back to just the day before, when she had been homeless – a day when she had slept under a bridge, outside.

I asked Yvonne, "What was it like to live under the bridge?"

She replied, "No electricity under the bridge, no running water. Dirty. I mean, just dirt everywhere. Dirt in everything… I don't know, last night was strange. It was very quiet here. No trains. My toy train was gone. No traffic. The neighbors were quiet."

Yvonne's former "home" was near a railroad and was beneath a busy downtown bridge.

She continued, "If it wasn't for Christy this winter and Mission from Mars, we would have really been rough. It's no fun to go to the shelter. Because, look, I'm crazier than Cooter Brown, but there's some real crazy people out there. So, I ain't got nothing on crazy compared to some of them. But, everyone's gotta be a little bit crazy to survive, no matter what station in life they are in."

She proceeded to tell us about this big church that she had gone to downtown, a place with screens and videos, and a service experience unlike anything that she was used to. But she decided to stay, determined to get something from it.

She told us that the pastor said, "Wherever you are right now in life, your life has a shelf life. You will not stay there; you will move on. Whether it be up or down, you will move on. Whether it be up or down, that's your choice."

She then told us about a beggar in the story of Lazarus, who asked for a drop of water and received none. She described the homeless beggar and the rich man who had all that he desired, but went to hell.

And she said, "I'll be the homeless beggar anytime."

Yvonne was a bit hard to follow in her storytelling, but looking back, a lot of what she said was really profound. She realized what a gift her life was, and she even saw her homelessness as a gift.

I never considered that we would have a part, even a small one, in helping someone go from living on the streets to living in an apartment. I never dreamed how much I would learn from these very real people, people who have suffered and have used that suffering to teach others like me the value of "stuff."

When we asked Yvonne what kept her going, what allowed her to live on the street for over a year and a half, she replied, "There is no choice, lay down and die or keep going. I don't want to die; I'm not done yet."

Indeed, Yvonne has much more to teach.

Luke 16:19-31

The Parable of the Rich Man and Lazarus.

"There was a rich man - who dressed in purple garments and fine linen and dined sumptuously each day. And lying at his door was a poor man named Lazarus, covered with sores, who would gladly have eaten his fill of the scraps that fell from the rich man's table. Dogs even used to come and lick his sores. When the poor man died, he was carried away by angels to the bosom of Abraham. The rich man also died and was buried, and from the netherworld, - where he was in torment, he raised his eyes and saw Abraham far off and Lazarus at

his side. And he cried out, 'Father Abraham, have pity on me. Send Lazarus to dip the tip of his finger in water and cool my tongue, for I am suffering torment in these flames. Abraham replied, 'My child, remember that you received what was good during your lifetime while Lazarus likewise received what was bad; but now he is comforted here, whereas you are tormented. Moreover, between us and you a great chasm is established to prevent anyone from crossing who might wish to go from our side to yours or from your side to ours. He said, 'Then I beg you, father, send him to my father's house, for I have five brothers, so that he may warn them, lest they too come to this place of torment. But Abraham replied, 'They have Moses and the prophets. Let them listen to them. He said, 'Oh no, father Abraham, but if someone from the dead goes to them, they will repent. Then Abraham said, 'If they will not listen to Moses and the prophets, neither will they be persuaded if someone should rise from the dead.'''

Chapter 12

A MOVEMENT

"Be you. Be what you can be today. Be Encouraging. Be Present. Be Thankful. Be Changed. Be Kind. Be Love. Be Authentic. Be Generous. Be Creative. Be Strong. Be Hopeful. Be a Friend. Be Compassionate. Be Daring. Be Enough. Be part of something bigger than yourself."

Natalie

We had delivered our first Welcome Wagons and our excitement continued to build. We wanted everyone to share in this incredible experience and to stay engaged. With summer travel and sports, we knew it would be hard to keep the same level of commitment as many in our group had families and children.

Natalie:

May 26, 2016

So many exciting things happening. Please read and like if you read!!

1. Scroll and find the posts and video about the Welcome Wagon showing up at Yvonne's new place. Like them, love them (so they float to the top).

2. Stay tuned over the next few days on the vision for this group. It is going to BE Amazing and BE Fun. And I cannot wait for you to BE part of it.

IMPORTANT MESSAGE: Some may watch the videos and say "I wish I could do more. I wish I could be more, and give more, and help more. I want to be crystal clear: Days like today can only be done when we are all part of this team. It's not one person, it's a movement of lots of people in the same direction (think Nemo). It was about time, money, thoughts, talents, energy, EVEN liking posts to give someone encouragement on a project and YOU ALL were part of this. And I want you to know that. The chicken noodle soup that was made by preschoolers, they might have saved Yvonne's life under the bridge when she was suffering from severe pneumonia. Your towels that you washed, donated, folded, bagged - these will be the towels this woman uses. Your cards and notes give encouragement. Your donations of food, trash bags, plates, folding napkins, toiletries, gift cards, and more... ALL contribute to making a day like today happen.

So Be you. Be what you can be today. Be Encouraging. Be Present. Be Thankful. Be Changed. Be Kind. Be Love. Be Authentic. Be Generous. Be Creative. Be Strong. Be Hopeful. Be a Friend. Be Compassionate. Be Daring. Be Enough. Be part of something bigger than yourself.

As you can see, another vision for Under the Overpass was emerging, and it all began with Be. I should tell you that the "Interwoven Fabric Project" was an earlier version of this, which began with our core team - as we were interweaving our lives within the community. The name was almost universally panned by the group. Natalie was not deterred and challenged us to come up with something better. Someone suggested the Be Something

Project, like Be Kind, Be Helpful, Be Whatever you could think of. The name stuck.

The Be Project gave us the flexibility to BE whatever we wanted to be! BE prepared, there will BE a lot more puns and double references.

<u>Natalie:</u>

May 26, 2016

Several of us have been thinking about where we go with this group and have come up with a vision. We are a group that makes dreams happen. Together as a team, we are doing awesome things, that one person just can't do. So I introduce to you.... The Be _____ Project Vision....

The Be _____ Project started in 2016. It wasn't a project, it was a bunch of friends, neighbors and strangers who were all different. They came together from different backgrounds, different interests, different groups of friends, different hobbies, different talents, different time constraints, different sports teams, different dreams, different beliefs, different churches and different faiths.
But they were amazing together. They are going to change their community together.
They were being... being thoughtful, being loving, being generous, being fun, being helpful, being amazing, being hospitable, being kind. So we decided to create a movement and transform this group into change makers. To encourage each of them to BE a leader and BE part of something bigger than themselves.
Be Love.
Be Silly.
Be Kind.
Be a Friend.

Be a part of something bigger than yourself.
Be _____.

Welcome. Thanks for jumping on a moving train. YOU are now
part of the BE team. (We are the A team.... don't BE Confused).

Stay Tuned and follow along. I think you'll catch on quick. I
encourage you to set this page as a favorite and also receive
notifications. I BElieve this is going to BE Big. This is going to be a
place where everyone is going to BElong.

Natalie wanted to affirm the incredible work that was going on and make sure that everyone, for their small or large roles, were feeling like they had contributed. There were also some among the group who wanted to do more in terms of volunteerism and engagement, and not all of the things they wanted to do related to the homeless. Some had a heart for children and began collecting backpacks for school kids in need. Others supported youth shelters and centers nearby. Our interests and passions were varying, but we were also bound together by a common interest in helping in our community. This flexible thinking also encouraged projects like the Welcome Wagon, which were independently led.

The posts by Natalie in the Be Project group after the visit to Yvonne's house were meant to inspire, to motivate, to help move people to action. One of the problems in any group is that most people don't see themselves as leaders. We often define leaders as those who do big things, but we were looking for each person to do small, but impactful things.

We don't think that the towels we folded or the notes we gave will have an impact. But, seeing Yvonne open a card that one of my kids made... seeing the tears that the card brought, that someone cared about her, the card wasn't just a card. The card and the towels, they are a way to bring joy, compassion, and care - a way of showing love for each other.

The lyrics for Josh Wilson's, *Dream Small* song really captures the importance of the little things.

**Dream small
Don't bother like you've gotta do it all
Just let Jesus use you where you are
One day at a time
Live well
Loving God and others as yourself
Find little ways where only you can help
With His great love
A tiny rock can make a giant fall
Dream small**

Natalie:

May 26, 2016

Is everyone still with me? Or did your dreaming get deflated by making dinner or cleaning or volunteering or working out or getting kids off the bus?

I would like to launch the "Be _____" project. Looking for input on the name. Be something bigger than yourself project. Be Bigger.

We launch the project with Tammy in the lead. She is "Be Kind" and we are going to help her make this dream happen. We will do a big kindness day where we collect Walmart gift cards and her kids will run up to someone with balloons and use the gift cards to pay their bill. We will also launch a be kind month - where everyone signs up for a random act of kindness.

Ok - so - what will you BE today?

Be something bigger than yourself

Comments:

Allison: *This whole thread made me laugh out loud....BE YOU!!!!*

Rita: *We need to schedule you a spa day Natalie, you need some relaxation time off.*

Gigi: *I'm digging it - the movement, the ideas, the concept...*

And so our first month of The BE Project had come to a close! And we chose BE KIND to kick it all off! We sent Natalie to the spa to regain her sanity, and we trudged on!

Our first official Be Project was to fulfill Tammy's dream.

Natalie's posts continued that same day…

Five hours later. As you can see, she never rests. Natalie believes that if she is doing God's work, he multiplies her time. Given her output, I am 100% certain he does!

Natalie:

May 26, 2016

I believe leaders are not born. There are some things in common and some skills that are needed, but I think one of the biggest factors is the choice. **The decision to lead.**

I do not believe "The Be _____ Project" (formerly known as Under the Overpass) can ever be 'managed.' It just cannot be a factory where top/down we tell people what to do and make cookbooks and detailed how-to's. It needs to be led by leaders, horizontally. I know people want the 'to do's'. But unless leaders step up, it's not sustainable to manage.

Paraphrased from Seth Godin Ted/Tribes author....
"The nature of leadership is that you're not doing what's been done before. If you were, you'd be following, not leading."

Are there thousands of reasons why you, of all people, aren't the right one to lead something right now? You don't have the time, resources, authority, genes or momentum? Probably. You still get to make the choice.

You can choose to lead, or not. You can choose to have faith, or not. You can choose to contribute to the tribe, or not.

Once you choose to lead, you'll be under huge pressure to reconsider your choice, to compromise, to dumb it down, or to give up.

You all have a BE passion. Don't do it alone. Throw a rock in the pond and let's share it. You are passionate about kids, allergies, health, teaching, sports, organizing, kindness, cooking, eating, love, friendship, education, reading.... let's get other people involved in your passion!

Your job this month: Encourage others, like posts, explain to friends, get others involved, do a random act of kindness this month and take a picture and tell people you did it… because this month is "Be Kind." Give a gift card.

Natalie sent us YouTube videos on the making of a movement and encouraged the team to move forward with us, to find and fuel their own passions.

We were involving people from all over our city, and they were thrilled to take on small and big roles to help out. We were giving people a way to serve, and they were excited about it. We were riding the momentum of our first two Welcome Wagons. New people were stepping up to schedule Sunday lunches, and then we got some even better news from Christy…

Christy *added* _new photos._

May 24, 2016

For those of you that know Major (the man who had been helping Natalie distribute Bibles to the camps), I am ecstatic the VA got him in a place for one year paid within 2 months of the application (Major is a veteran)!!! He has been in Pittsburgh on the streets since February. When I met him in the emergency shelter I thought he was a social worker for Operation Safety Net! I about died when I found out he was homeless. He has been the sharpest dressed homeless man around Pittsburgh.

He is taking in the female who has been under the bridge with him. The below tent has been their home. I am so happy for Major, he didn't want to be out there.

Along with her post, Christy included pictures of Major's old "residence."

Homeless camp area in the woods on riverbank

She also included a picture of the rear hatch of her vehicle, "filled" with a meager bag of items to be transported to Major's new home. There was a backpack and two sleeping bags, one that was his, and one for the woman he was taking in with him. Natalie gave a quick rehash of Major's story to our group:

Natalie:

May 24, 2016

For those of you that have heard 'the rest of the story' of The Bible Project - Major is my homeless friend who would deliver my Bibles under the bridges when I had to take a break in the spring. He also would send me prayer requests from his neighbors on the streets and we would share encouragement while reading through Paul Tripp's New Morning Mercies devotional. He's gone through a lot and will continue to face struggles as he gets back on his feet, but I'm thankful that he will have an opportunity for a fresh start. Please pray for him as he tries to rebuild.

Heading into summer, we were thrilled with the progress that was made. So much was happening, so many volunteers were getting involved, Mission from Mars was growing, and it looked like a new ministry was about to take off, the Welcome Wagon.

Chapter 13

CHRISTY

"'For it is in giving that we receive.'"

Saint Francis of Assisi

In the short seven months Christy had been serving the homeless, she began to have a loyal following. Mission from Mars went viral and word had spread that special things were happening with the group. Recognition came in the form of a nomination for the Locker Room Leadership Award.

Natalie *shared* **_Christy's post:_**

May 23, 2016

This is from Christy. (Christy had shared a screenshot that included the following information about the nomination):

> *"Dear Christy,*
>
> *Congratulations! You have been nominated for the Locker Room Leadership Award. This award is given annually by sports broadcasters and former Steelers Tunch Ilkin and Craig Wolfley and Light of Life Rescue Mission. It recognizes people like you who have*

gone above and beyond to help the poor and homeless in Pittsburgh. Thank you!

We would be honored if you would join us for an award ceremony which will take place on Friday, May 27 at 9:30 am in Market Square (in downtown Pittsburgh). Dennis Bowman will be the emcee and Tunch and Wolf will be on hand as well as staff from Light of Life Rescue Mission, to celebrate your exemplary work to combat homelessness in Pittsburgh."

Christy: *feeling honored:*

May 18 at 7:47pm

Alright who did it!!! Nothing like disregarding what I thought was spam and apparently I have been nominated for an award. Thank goodness she called me too! How sweet is that!!! Who did it!!??

The big day had come for Christy, and a few of us decided to go with her to the award ceremony downtown. It was a great way to support Christy, a survivor who had been through so much and had begun her ascent from despair. It was the middle of the workday, but a large crowd had assembled. Christy was excited to see so many of our core team and so many of her homeless friends. Mark was there and Yvonne and at least five more of our homeless and formerly homeless friends. We all gathered together to excitedly cheer her award. We knew the effort, sacrifice, and hard work that was being recognized.

The award was a great affirmation for the entire Mission from Mars community, and it also drove new volunteers to the mission. Some leaders from The Be Project group were stepping up into "leadership roles" within Mission from Mars. Meals were still being served each week, even through the summer, and new people were coming to help.

As summer turned to fall, Mission from Mars was running entirely on its own with its own volunteers. Meal schedules were posted online and community groups like the Boy and Girl Scouts, sports teams, and community service groups were booking dates to cook and serve.

The Be Project was allowing us the freedom to support some other charitable causes as well, particularly The Bible Project and the Welcome Wagon ministries. The Bible Project had taken on new members who wanted to adopt the project in their own hometowns. It eventually spread throughout the country and even to countries around the world. Natalie was engaging new leaders within this ministry, who were spreading the Word far and wide.

Natalie was focusing more and more of her efforts on building the Bible Project, while continuing to follow along with Mission from Mars. As the months passed, and winter came for our second season of coordinated efforts with Mission from Mars, the Be Project was now a fully prepared, albeit loosely organized group.

People wanting to bring food for Mission from Mars reserved dates online, read the "manuals," and brought food and volunteers. Christy continued to show up on Sundays with her team, and the meals were now well known throughout the homeless community. In my role with the church, I was able to recruit and send teams to serve. The church became a new channel for people to be involved and even prepare food.

We were beginning our next phase as Be Project Members.

Jen:

July 26, 2016

So today was really amazing! I met Tom Mitlo, founder of The Blessing Board, at the Oakmont location. Their warehouse is HUGE! They have so many beds, dressers, etc. and they have them all very neatly arrayed. They collect anything you would need for a house - with the following caveat...if your house burned in a fire, what would you truly need? No knick knacks, but yes, towels and kitchen wares. They are in desperate need of towels right now. Each family can choose 5 large items and a few other household items (linens, kitchen utensils, dishes, etc.). Things like vacuum cleaners are in short supply. They also take appliances.

On Sunday September 25, our church will host a donation drive where we try to stock their warehouse. They get over 600 requests per month, but can only accommodate about 100. I met 10 Somali refugees who were there today, and even interviewed the translator (a refugee herself who has also used The Blessing Board). Very sad stories of the utter disregard for human life that they have endured.

The Blessing Board also helps lots of domestic violence victims, the homeless (who have keys to a home) and others.

So, I was thinking - what if we kick start the fall with The BE PROJECT by being kind and supporting this event? Our group can contribute whatever we have to donate to the donation drive (you will only need to get stuff to the church, not all the way to the warehouse). They also accept cash contributions. Feel free to invite friends and to drop off - hours will be 10 am-2 pm.

Want to go a mile further? Consider offering your truck to help your family or friends get their items to the drop off point.

And for those looking for a volunteer opportunity- it's a really great place with a good message. Even our group of Muslim refugees received a Christian message explaining why the volunteers were helping them and doing this for them. Feel free to contact Blessing Board directly if you want to volunteer.

Learning about some of the services that were available for our friends helped us do a better job connecting and supporting them. In the meantime, another Welcome Wagon was given for a woman named Trish. She had been featured in the news in 2015 as a person who had aged out of the foster care system and landed on the street.

Tammy shared with us a link to the newspaper article about Trish. She was a regular at our lunches and a friend of Christy's:

"Downtown Pittsburgh center to serve youths aging out of foster care"

Natasha Lyndstrom

PittsburghTribuneReview.com

Friday, Dec. 25, 2015, 9:42 p.m.

<u>*Profile of a homeless child*</u>

Allegheny County surveyed 56 homeless children and adults younger than 24 to learn more about their circumstances. Here are the findings:

• 53 percent — Have a history of physical, emotional or sexual trauma

• 51 percent — Have been in foster care

• 34 percent — Do not have a high school diploma

• 33 percent — Have been to jail or prison

• *32 percent — Identify as asexual, bisexual, gay, lesbian, pansexual or other*

• *29 percent — Have been in juvenile detention*

• *27 percent — Have a child of their own*

• *8 percent — Identify as genderqueer, transgender or other*

Source: Allegheny County Department of Human Services, Youth Count 2015

Patricia Todd doesn't think about her turbulent childhood often, mostly because she wants to keep the painful past behind her.

Many early memories blur together. Her first, at about 5, elicits feelings of unfamiliarity and anxiety in a cramped living space shared by a dozen girls at a Southern California group home, one in a string of so many stints in foster care that Todd lost count.

From 6 months until her 17th birthday, while bouncing among foster families, relatives, friends and her abusive father's custody, Todd says, she rarely had privacy or quiet moments to herself.

Yet mostly, she recalls feeling alone.

"I was very shy and very quiet," the soft-spoken 27-year-old said from her latest temporary home, a partitioned room in Bethlehem Haven's women's shelter in Pittsburgh's Uptown. "Growing up, I didn't really know anywhere I could go."

Todd's experience of isolation is common for children in the foster care system and neglectful households — a population at major risk of a litany of problems later in life…

Todd — healing from verbal, physical and sexual abuse inflicted by family and strangers — said she wishes a teacher, counselor or role model had attempted to get her to open up about her tumultuous home life.

"Nobody really tried to do that with me, and it made me feel very lonely," Todd said.

Nearly a decade after child protective workers removed her from her father's custody for good when she reported that he choked her, Todd found herself in another abusive relationship. A loud dispute with her boyfriend got her evicted last year from the apartment she was renting in Squirrel Hill.

She packed up what she had, put it into a storage unit she paid for with federal disability checks and spent the next several months living on the street and sleeping on the sofas in friends' houses.

In her sixth month at Bethlehem Haven's women's shelter, Todd is optimistic she won't be there much longer. She meets three times a week with a coach who helps her with a job hunt and holds her accountable. She's awaiting word on jobs at Giant Eagle and Taco Bell, but ultimately wants to get nursing certification. Her dream is to find a career working with children, animals or seniors.

She's eager to have her own place again, hopefully within the next three months.

"I've already been here too long," she said.

After learning about Trish's story, we were all onboard to help her in any way we could. It was awesome to see that her dream of getting her own place was coming true.

Tammy *is with* *Christy*.

July 29, 2016 · Pittsburgh

Trish in her new home. Thanks to all of YOU who donated pots and pans, sheets, comforters, towels, pillows, plates, paper products, filled laundry baskets with cleaning supplies and all sorts of goodies, etc. I must say today had a different feel.

This apartment had no steps in the front and we had to carry everything up two steep flights of stairs around the back. Her toilet does not flush. There is no A/C. Stuff was just laying on the ground. She has been to the Blessing Board and had a small tv and a bunch of pantry items, a few books and some clothing and a few pieces of furniture.

There was litter outside and boarded up windows in the apartment below her. I called her landlord to try to get her toilet fixed and he insisted it was simply a plunging issue (which it is not and her place had a faint odor to it).

My heart aches for her and people like her. I have so many mixed emotions--so glad a group like ours can help people out there and that she has a place to call her own, but also so sad that we are only catching a glimpse of the real suffering out there. Keep up those prayers, my friends!!! You are doing good things!

We were technically "on a break" from serving the Sunday lunch (Ross and Rachel from *Friends* reference intended), but we didn't always stay away. Summer, it seemed, was almost as difficult for our friends as winter!

Jen:

July 31, 2016

A really long line came out for delicious eats by <u>Laura</u> and <u>Lisa</u>! Great job! I have to say, summer serving was more heart wrenching than winter. Many begged for deodorant. The smells were not pleasant and the group seemed even less happy. The effects of the brutally hot sun were evident. One man had a wet towel on his head. Being homeless sucks.

We will be making blessing bags at our Outreach Summer Camp (I had planned a full week of outreach activities for kids to help those in need) Aug 8 to pass out with MFM. Such a tough life for so many, so many needs. Thanks for being an amazing group I'm proud to know!

As the summer went on, more Welcome Wagons were happening, keeping Tammy and Gigi's team busy!

Tammy:

August 5, 2016

Rich and Carol are in their home!! Welcome Wagon scheduled for Sunday August 21st. Anyone available? Thinking we can go after Sunday lunch around 1.

AND...Even more Welcome Wagons

Tammy:

November 18, 2016

WHAT A MORNING!!! Two Welcome Wagons distributed to our friends Tito and Elon. Huge thank you to all who contributed the many, many goodies for these folks and especially to Gigi and Christy (and my sidekick, Ryan aka Booty) for making the rounds with me today. Tito had been in his apartment for two weeks and his apartment was bare. You could tell he had been cleaning it...it was spotless and smelled so clean, and he had a small radio going when we got there. But there was nothing....not even a pot or a pan, or a plate, or a piece of furniture. His joy just took over and he was overwhelmed as he was looking through the laundry baskets, bag of pots and pans, sheets, towels, etc.

One of Christy's friends met us there and unloaded boxes of canned goods. Gigi helped him put the plates and utensils away, and hung up his new shower curtain. He gave us a full tour of his apartment and was telling us how he someday wanted to furnish his home with a baby grand piano! He loves to play classical music. Gigi is working on getting him an electric keyboard for now :) Tito was also talking about wanting to start a program to help beautify his new neighborhood.

This man had been in prison and had been homeless since he got out. He applied for his own Section 8 housing and obtained this home on his own without any help. Christy, of course, was armed with all her resources and contact information for him to get a bed, some furniture, boots for the winter, etc.

We rummaged through our pockets to get him some quarters as he was so excited that the laundry mat was only 6 blocks away. We also provided him with a bus pass to help him get around town, and some chicken, mashed potatoes, and apple dumplings for a nice warm dinner. He hugged us and thanked us and none of us wanted to leave!

We then headed to McKees Rocks to see Elon. Christy was unable to reach him by phone, but we showed up and he was there. I had met Elon at lunch on Sunday, and he had requested tilapia for one of his first home cooked meals....so tilapia he received, along with some mashed potatoes, dumplings and a salad. Elon has been in his new home for about two months after living in his church's basement about 10 blocks away. Elon can pay for his rent and utilities with the little bit of social security he receives each month, and he had a few bucks leftover to purchase some pieces of used furniture. He had a small table and four chairs, an old couch, and a bookshelf.

Elon has two bad knees and is having a biopsy on Monday on a tumor that the doctors found in his leg....so please, extra prayers for our buddy. Our team carried all of his items in for him, and got to work quickly putting things away in his kitchen, hanging up his shower curtain, etc. We noticed that his fire alarms were beeping, signaling that the batteries were old. Gigi insisted that we go buy him some new batteries and change them out immediately! We left to go to the Dollar Store and grabbed him the batteries, some new light bulbs for his bedroom lamp, and some supplies for him to clean his floors (Elon's request as he wanted to clean his floors himself!). We brought the items back to his home, and luckily his landlord happened to be there, so he fixed Elon's smoke detectors for him. We then said our goodbyes and headed back home.

I hope you ALL know what a difference you are making in others' lives, just by being who you are and doing the wonderful things you are doing. Please continue to pray for our homeless friends and for those who have recently obtained housing.

Comments:

Gigi: *Tito got his keyboard today after Sunday lunch! He was thrilled and played me a few tunes! Elon showed up at lunch today and looked so nice, he dressed up for the occasion and was smiling ear to ear! He's still talking about your tilapia!*
There's lots of work to do, but good things are happening....The MOVEMENT Has Begun!

While still infrequent, people began getting off the streets and into housing. We truly didn't expect it, but were thrilled to witness this change. We began earnestly collecting for more Welcome Wagons and soon our next delivery appointment had arrived.

This was our first trip to the McKeesport area, and we were meeting Ronald, who had been a regular at the lunches. Christy and I brought the items indoors, while Tammy and little Booty, her son, stayed in the car. I wrote an article about our experience for our church bulletin not long after the delivery:

The FrostBite Lottery

Imagine the feeling of winning the lottery. The excitement you would feel at being the person selected to receive a huge payday. You are now living at the Ritz, living the high life. You might describe a surreal feeling, one of non-belief that this has really happened to you. This is how Ronald described his life change to me, only he didn't win the lottery. Instead, he was selected for one of just a dozen or so housing slots that provide not just housing, but supportive care as well. Ronald is free to stay as long as he wishes in the complex, where they offer help with tasks as simple as grocery shopping.

What led Ronald to this point in his life where he effectively won the lottery? The tale begins over 25 years ago, when Ronald first landed on the streets. It's hard to picture a person living outdoors for so long, but that is all part of his story. Most recently he was living in the woods, where he was using a tarp as protection from the elements. Ronald's clothing, his torn pants and tattered shirt, show just how far he has come now that he is in a new residence. They are a visual indication of where he has been. Looking at his disheveled, long, gray hair, you might avoid him if you saw him on the street, but his mild, meek voice shows the gentleness that is within. He walks with a cane and the dressings on his foot remind him of how close he was to losing his limb.

So how did Ronald end up living the high life? It happened in an unexpected way. Ronald's hand had turned black and frostbite had set in to both his hand and foot. He went to the Emergency Room where they gave him basic treatment, but not having any insurance, they sent him on his way. They were nice enough to give him cab fare, sending him to Light of Life Mission, where he was entered into a system which helps the homeless secure housing. You might be wondering; does he abuse alcohol or drugs? Perhaps surprisingly, the answer is no, he does not.

After a short stay at Light of Life, Ronald's number was drawn in the proverbial lottery and he was offered the chance to live indoors after so many years. He jumped at the chance and is now living a dream in a small, clean, one bedroom apartment in urban Pittsburgh. Ronald has a long way to go to recover from the trauma that living outdoors for so long can inflict, but for now he is on top of the world.

I implored our church community to get more involved in volunteering with our area's homeless.

And then the Christmas season came!

Natalie:

December 6, 2016

All - _Christy from Mission from Mars is collecting $5 gift cards to McDonald's to give out at Christmas. If you would like to donate, you can get to me, Jena, Gigi and anyone else who wants to comment to be a collector. Great opportunity to gather if you have any parties coming up._

From Christy: _If you can buy a homeless person dinner $5 at McDonalds, please shoot me some gift cards. It is a Christmas gift and I would like to have one for as many as I can reach. 25 women's emergency shelter (Mission Accomplished!) + 8 in camp (Mission Accomplished!) + 75 at our lunch. I would like to do 115 guys in the emergency shelter too. Go big or go home kind of girl I am. And really....having lost another one of my guys, I don't know what else to do except work for them right now._

Christy's campaign was successful and a gift card was provided to each and every one at Christmas. A very special gift for all, but her heart was heavy. She had recently lost a friend, a camp regular named Boston who had overdosed on drugs. It was tragic and many of our friends at lunch and behind the scenes were feeling the effects.

Chapter 14

FEAR

"What you are afraid to do is a clear indication of the next thing you need to do."

Ralph Waldo Emerson

Summer and fall came and went, and with it so did more Welcome Wagons. What we thought might never be replicated, people getting off the streets and into housing, was happening at an even faster rate. Tammy and Gigi had adopted this ministry as their own. They had been collecting donations in their basements and garages, often to the chagrin of their husbands. For the most part, the men were good sports and didn't say much about parking the car outside or having to navigate more carefully in their basements. Entire families were contributing by putting up with some minor inconveniences in support of the mission.

The Welcome Wagon was growing and had been a blessing to the formerly homeless community for over a year. The team had helped 10 people get into housing and provided them with all manner of household and kitchen furnishings. Tammy, Booty, and Gigi, along with Christy, had been on most of these deliveries. There were two Welcome Wagons scheduled for this day, and Tammy asked me to ride along.

Something about it felt off for me. As I did with Yvonne's Welcome Wagon, I began to feel very nervous.

Have you ever felt fear, real, true fear? The kind that activates your fight or flight mechanisms, the kind that stands the hairs on your neck and creates a feeling of anxiety throughout your entire body? That kind of fear? That's how I felt getting ready for this Welcome Wagon.

The two appointments were with Marlon and Mike, two men I had never met before. We would be headed to Etna and Braddock, both outside of the city of Pittsburgh. In Etna, I knew what to expect. Its old, dated homes and many row houses have been repeatedly damaged by floods as many of these homes are built too close to the river behind them. When the banks overflow, the homes are often flooded, and the people are left with a house full of water, or worse, mold. For some, the homes are uninsurable. For many others, they are left vacant, leaving dilapidated structures behind. But it wasn't the Etna delivery I was worried about.

I was worried about the first delivery. I knew very little about the town, but my only encounters there had been extremely negative. The drive was about an hour from our suburban dwellings where we packed up the "loot" collected by Tammy and Gigi. There were televisions, pots, pans, houseware items, silverware, and of course, the hot meal…a Welcome Wagon staple. But my worries about the location stemmed from earlier visits where, during broad daylight, it appeared no one worked. I had visited Braddock on a couple of occasions for a prior job and was anxious to leave both times.

There is something unsettling about seeing large groups of people of working age milling about outside, loitering really, and doing absolutely nothing mid-day. It's the kind of loitering that can lead to trouble, and I had no interest in going back.

When I told Tammy I would help with the Welcome Wagon, I thought we were just doing one in Etna. They added the second one at the last minute, excited that another of our friends was getting into housing. But now the terms had changed, and I didn't feel like I could back out.

As I prepared to leave my house, the text streams began. Christy was feeling ill and was dealing with personal issues. She asked "if we would mind if she didn't join us."

Yes! We mind! You're the tough guy (gal) of this operation! How could you not come with us? How could you send us to this neighborhood on our own?

These were the thoughts running through my head as I reread her text.

Gigi coolly texted back, "No problem. We've got this."

I followed suit, knowing just how much Christy had done and that she really deserved a break. It didn't stop me from letting the group know of my concerns.

"Does anyone have pepper spray they can bring?"

The group text, which included myself, Christy, Tammy, Natalie, and Gigi, was not reassuring. (Natalie enjoyed staying in tune to our goings-on, and also acted as our de facto call-the-police-if-something-bad-happened person. She was always on-call from the friendly confines of home.)

Tammy didn't have any pepper spray and her husband was concerned about this delivery. "Maybe we should bring a knife?" Tammy texted.

I wanted to reply that you don't bring a knife to a gun fight, but that seemed a little excessive for the moment.

Gigi assured us she could handle herself, and our fates were sealed. Tammy, Gigi, and I would do the deliveries. Have you ever seen the movie *Rudy* where the groundskeeper tells him, "you're five-foot nuthin, a hundred and nuthin?" That's what was running through my mind. These two couldn't be a hundred pounds each sopping wet and they certainly weren't much over five feet tall!

Gigi messaged that she would bring her switchblade comb, which she was sure would be mistaken for the real thing in case of a problem. Tammy promised to bring her stinky pits, she had just finished working out. With that, our futures were in the hands of a pretend tough girl and a hugger. I still laugh when thinking about the pictures of deodorant spray and smelly armpits that were being texted, or the *Grease* era switchblade comb pictures sent my way. These girls were hysterical!

Anxiously, I left my driveway to meet Tammy and Gigi to deliver two Welcome Wagons for people who were no longer living on the street.

Christy's last text, "Remember, we are the food and the love ladies….We are protected and have the armor of God."

I was definitely hoping God was paying attention and had the armor out, but the fact that even Christy was thinking about safety had me even more nervous.

As we drove, we bantered back and forth about the latest diets. Tammy was doing a juice cleanse and was completely stressed at work. Her phone kept chiming texts from the "Crazy Cleansers," the name of her group of friends who were also only sipping juices in an effort to lose the dreaded holiday pounds. Gigi was also cleansing, and she described her diet in terms of organic chicken recipes and wholesome veggies. I couldn't help but be struck by the two different worlds I was living in. One, with the Crazy Cleansers and my suburban friends - where our lives involve trips to Whole Foods and the gym. The other, well, I was headed to the other world at that very moment – to the places where those lucky enough to get off the street would find shelter - even if those shelters weren't something I would want to live in.

My fears actually subsided as we drove. I was pleasantly surprised to find no one loitering near the front of the building when we arrived. We called Marlon on the phone and asked him to come downstairs. He was living in a converted building, some sort of quasi public housing facility. With the minivan stuffed full, along with three very female faces, we stood out like sore thumbs.

Undeterred, we began unloading in front of the building. We had dishes, silverware, and some great cookware. We were told Marlon really liked to cook, so he got all brand new items. He greeted us at the door with a huge smile and was anxious to get his new things to his room.

In the front entry we found a manned reception desk and a placard that said to "sign in." As we approached, the girl at the desk looked at us quizzically. Apparently it isn't every day that the movers show up for the newly housed. She quickly called over the facilities director, who asked who we were and what we were doing there. Tammy grabbed her hand and introduced herself.

"We're the Welcome Wagon from Mission from Mars."

The look on the Director's face was priceless. Completely blank.

"Never heard of it," she said in a completely deadpan voice.

I imagined her saying, "Of course you are, dear." In this building and in this setting, it sounded hilarious in my mind.

Tammy, with her infectious smile was undeterred. "We're just here to give Marlon some stuff for his new place."

Same voice in my head repeated itself, "Of course you are."
People were looking at us like we were crazy.

A voice in the background said she would take the items to the hot room.

"The what," I asked?

The voice had come from the receptionist and she was preparing to take all of Marlon's worldly belongings (which was now everything we had carried into the facility) to the hot room.

"The hot room gets to 150 degrees," explained the Director, as if I could understand why on earth we would want to almost boil Marlon's new pots and pans.

"We have a real problem with bed bugs here, so anything that isn't brand new or could bring in bed bugs goes in the hot room first."

Wow! I was not expecting that! When I began to think about it, it made sense because the homeless population battles bedbugs.

I showed the Director the new pots and pans and slightly hid the pillow and bedding. "This all came out of her house (pointing to Tammy). It's safe. You don't have to worry," I said.

She looked at Tammy and her designer coat and sunglasses and obviously realized the risk of bed bugs was low.

"They're OK. Looks like all the stuff is brand new," she told the receptionist.

At that, Marlon, who was very anxious to get upstairs, asked the Director if we could join him.

"Only two can go up at a time, and the boy can't go," said the Director.

It was about this moment that I realized we had brought Tammy's four year old son to the homeless shelter. I know this realization should have dawned on me much earlier, but the look on the Director's face that screamed, "What on earth are you idiots doing bringing a little boy into a homeless shelter" reminded me.

Yeah, that look. That's what made me remember this quiet little guy was still with us. While it wasn't technically a homeless shelter, it wasn't exactly neighborhood apartments either.

"I'll stay with Booty," I volunteered, wanting no part of going upstairs with Marlon. Very quickly, Tammy shot me down immediately. She would stay with her son and the relative safety of the Director.

As we loaded a small cart with items for Marlon, we were suddenly very aware that every eye in the entire center was watching us. There was a sitting room off the entrance and there were 10-15 men just hanging out - staring intently at us. I don't think there was a TV and they certainly weren't working or playing any sort of games. They were simply sitting there and watching us, obviously the entertainment of the day. It was unnerving and the butterflies were back in my stomach.

Unfortunately, we still had to retrieve some items from the car to complete the Welcome Wagon. While the car was only parked across the street, none of us were all that excited to go back to it. When we had pulled in, a man had come up next to us and simply stood and stared at us. He was dressed in a very bulky coat and was obviously a big man. Initially he was on his phone, but then he simply watched us unload the car. There was a parking garage ramp directly next to us. When he heard the high-pitched wail of an ambulance approaching, he coolly stepped into the garage, almost as if he wanted to avoid being seen. Not helping my creepy crawly feeling. I couldn't unload, as I refused to look away from the man staring at us so intently. I grabbed a small handful from the trunk and little Booty to get him inside where it was warm. Gigi and Tammy promised to be quickly behind, but in their haste had gotten something stuck on the hatch of the van. Tammy could not get it closed and she was almost panicked. Gigi, hands full, couldn't help, so I gave her Booty and went back to help.

Calmly, I told Tammy, "Let's get inside."

On the inside, I was screaming, "hurry the xyz up! Don't you know this guy is staring us up and down and looks like he wants to do bad things! Let's go! Who cares if we give this guy any more stuff."

But I didn't say any of those things. Instead, I put my brave ninja face on, grabbed a toaster from Tammy, and helped her close the trunk. Finally, we were all inside.

While it felt good to get away from the creepy guy, who was alternating between lurking in the parking garage and within a few feet of the car, we now got to enter the fishbowl which was the reception area again. All eyes were again trained on us. You know how when you go to a restaurant and see a celebrity or someone you know and you tell your friend - "Hey, don't look but there's Brad Pitt in the corner over there." In this scenario, your friend will wait for the opportune moment to catch a fleeting glimpse, being careful not to stare. This was the exact opposite. Not one among them was doing anything but flat out staring at us. I was now *almost* happy to be going with Gigi upstairs to the stranger Marlon's room.

The elevator arrived and we said our goodbyes to Tammy and Booty, who had the enviable position of walking into the Director's office. We instead got to share a cramped elevator with a man neither one of us knew. Christy had asked Tammy and Gigi to do the Welcome Wagon for Marlon, but it was unclear how well she knew him.

But what Tammy and I didn't know until we left Marlon's, was that Gigi did know Marlon; she had met him before at the lunch and he scared the bejeezus out of her!

She met him during the summer and had asked him if there was anything she could get for him. He was standing across the street from where we would serve, simply staring at everyone eating.

His reply caught her off guard, "You get me a house?" he said in a snarky tone.

"No, but I can introduce you to Christy who can help get you to the right people," said Gigi cheerfully.

"You can't get me a house then you can't get me nuthin'. Go away!"

That was the comment Gigi was remembering as we were riding in a tiny elevator alone with Marlon. Her memory of him was that she was completely terrified! It would have been nice to have known that this was the guy we were doing the Welcome Wagon for before we got there!

Making small talk, Gigi said to Marlon that they met once before. She asked him if he remembered her. He did not. He talked about the bus pass that Tammy had given him last Sunday at lunch that was supposed to have $5 on it, but in fact was empty. He really wanted that bus pass. And "did you bring that Giant Eagle card (a local grocery store gift card)?"

No, we hadn't brought a Giant Eagle card. Actually, Gigi had planned to bring one but had forgotten. In the car on the ride there, it was decided that grocery cards would not be given to anyone who we thought was a smoker, as we didn't want food money going to cigarettes. We all agreed that we were too cheap to smoke at over $6/pack, but many of the homeless do smoke. We couldn't wrap our heads around how they could choose cigarettes over food, but addiction isn't easily broken.

As the elevator stopped at Marlon's floor, we began pushing the cart of stuff down the narrow hallway. There were doors lining the hall and there were a lot of them. I wondered to myself how many people live here, thinking the number had to be a lot given the number of doors. Marlon opened his locked door. The room was tiny. Not bedroom tiny. No, not even dorm room tiny. This was tiny on a much smaller scale. There was room for a single cot style bed, not even as wide as a standard single. The bed had a very simple frame and a window on the wall behind.

There was floor space that was roughly equivalent to the size of the bed and a tiny counter which held his crock pot. There was a small door, which I assumed led to a closet and that was it. All of the items we had brought upstairs filled the room quickly. Nothing hung on the wall; there was no color, or cheer, or happiness in the place. The bed was covered with a blue sleeping bag, which Marlon noticed me looking at.

"Slept in that for two years outside. Never once missed a shower. Every day, no matter how cold, I went and took a shower. Gotta take care of yourself out there," Marlon explained.

I had seen this before with Yvonne and Major, that the tent or sleeping bag, the most prized possession of the homeless, became a treasured item not to be parted with even once indoors. I wonder if there is always the fear that you will be outside again, and you wouldn't want to be without it. The uncertainty behind whether or not you would return to that life would be haunting.

"You know, you girls need to take care of yourselves out there. I watch you each week and you can't trust no one. That's what I do, I watch you. I'm taking care of you. There's bad people out there and you gotta watch."

Was this foreshadowing of our demise? Was Marlon one of these people?

He continued, "On the streets, sometimes you gotta do things you ain't proud of. Things to survive. I want to put all that past me. You know I have Crohn's disease. Don't have much of a colon left. Docs took it out. That's why I like to cook. Can't eat much, gotta be real careful. If I do, I'll pay."

Marlon looked the part of a survivor. He was fit and looked put together in his white Nike shirt and jacket and blue jeans. He had a tall frame, but was incredibly thin. He wore a stocking cap over his head even indoors and wore small, thin wire glasses. His pale skin and graying beard showed his age, I'm guessing late 60s. His features were rough and weathered.

Remembering Christy wanted us to get a picture, and realizing I really wanted to get out of Marlon's tiny room, I asked Marlon if he would mind if I took a picture. Gigi had been holding open the door to the room, and her eyes conveyed to me that I should not let the door close under any circumstance.

At that moment, a shadow appeared behind Gigi, and to hear her tell the story, this was the end in her mind. **And this is how it ends.** Stupid, minivan driving, switchblade comb wielding women pushed into ex-con's room. Our nerves were on high alert and our hearts were racing. She felt certain this shadowy figure was going to push her into the room, ending with our untimely demise.

As it turned out, the man was simply opening the door to his room, which was so close to Marlon's that it seemed like unsavory things were about to happen.

I offered to take the picture AND hold the door. I took the picture in a blink. Marlon had grabbed a pan we had brought and placed it under his arm for the photo. He was obviously very excited about his new stuff. He promised that he would cook every day in their common kitchen, where he can bring his cookware. Of course, he must bring it all back to his room or it would be stolen. But he was so glad to be able to cook for himself and his special dietary needs. He asked again about the gift card, saying how much he really wanted spices. Gigi said she would mail one to him.

As we walked back to the elevator with Marlon escorting us out, he stopped abruptly.

"Don't mail it here. You tell Christy, and I will get it from you at lunch. They look at everything here. That Director, she snoops. She's into my business. You send me that, you never know. Sticky fingers."

We let the idea of the staff here potentially taking things sink in.

We didn't know what to believe, but agreed that the gift card would be given in person. We collected Tammy and Booty from the Director's office and offered our thanks for her hospitality. Hugs were given to Marlon and as the entire living room crowd looked on, we were ready to walk to the car.

Seeing the man standing where we had left him next to our car, I asked Marlon if he would mind walking us out. He agreed without hesitation.

"Of course. You never can be too careful."

We were listening to his advice and he seemed glad to have taught us something. As we got into the car, more people approached, and the man did as well. We could hear the whirl of sirens in the distant background. None of us were feeling very comfortable and even Marlon looked a bit uneasy. Tammy was trying to buckle Booty's seat belt and just couldn't get it to clip, her hands likely a bit shaky. People were really close to us at this point and they didn't seem to have good intentions. Upstairs we had been petrified that something would happen, and now this...

After an excessive amount of fumbling with Booty's seat belt, I encouraged Tammy to let Gigi do it.

"Just get in the car and drive!" I said in a somewhat frantic voice.

Tammy instantly stopped, closed the doors and locked us in.

We waved goodbye to Marlon and the scary man staring at us on the street. Eventually, the little hairs on the back of my neck settled down.

At the end of the day, it seemed like Marlon was a pretty good guy who had been trying to protect us at the lunches and even in his new neighborhood. He had been through a lot, and we were glad to welcome him home.

We were now on to the next Welcome Wagon.

Chapter 15

MIKE ANTHONY

"Courage is knowing what not to fear."

Plato

In the car to deliver the next Welcome Wagon, we talked about why we were doing this - why we serve the homeless.

According to Tammy, "she just loves it," and this is exactly what she needs after the stressful week. I wanted to question if she was secretly working for the CIA or other high risk job, but knowing that she was an accountant, I couldn't quite comprehend how the Welcome Wagon could possibly be de-stressing!

Gigi donates part of her income from sales of cosmetic products each month to her work with the homeless. She seems to really enjoy knowing her work has a purpose, supporting the homeless.

I'm a little more cynical and often question the value of what we are doing. Some of the people we were meeting do drugs or hurt people; and sometimes, even after our best efforts to help them, they go back to their old ways.

It's draining to watch someone you have invested in personally get into housing and then lose it due to an inability to keep a job or manage finances. Yep, not that long after we had moved in one of our friends, she was asking for help moving out.

"Can you store my stuff?" she asked.

Seriously... store the stuff we gave you because you are being evicted? Store it because you aren't paying your rent, even though you were given money to do so? I thought.

It's so incredibly frustrating, but it's not uncommon for people to go back to what they know, which for some is panhandling for an existence. It seems unthinkable to me that anyone would consider panhandling an alternative to almost any other job. You have to sit outside, typically in the worst conditions, hoping for someone to have pity upon you. Some people will decidedly not have pity on you and will extol you to "Get a job" or "Do something with your life" among other insults. Or, they may physically assault you with spit or even a kick.

It does not appeal to me to fly the sign. But yet this is what some homeless do, even after getting into housing. It boggles my mind, but I am reminded not to judge. Never being in their shoes, I can't relate to the realities of this lifestyle.

So each time I lend a hand to the homeless, I'm filled with an inner conflict - a conflict where I know that some of the people we help are engaging in activities I don't agree with or that are illegal. They might be actively using drugs, stealing, or abusing someone else. Within our group, we have been disappointed to see monies used for drugs rather than a promised trip to see children. Or the $15 given for a bus pass or to get a driver's license, or any number of things, used for anything but.

Some people have tried to attach conditions to their money- "I will only give this to you if..." In my experience, this has rarely worked out. If someone is scheming money from you for drugs, they can be very persuasive and convincing, but in the end, if they are addicted they will still buy the drugs.

We drove to Etna after the first Welcome Wagon with Marlon. We left the first location intact and were eager to deliver the remaining goods. When we arrived at the house, we texted Mike to let him know we were there. Since he doesn't have phone service, we couldn't call. Our text unanswered, we proceeded to knock (let's be real, pound) on the row house door. No answer.

So we sat in the car and waited. We called Christy, who offered to try to help track him down. She assured us that she had spoken with him and made arrangements, although we were about an hour or two later than she had said. After much back and forth, we were unable to connect with him.

"Why don't you guys go into the bar across the street and see if they will hold it for you," offered Christy helpfully.

I say "helpfully" with sarcasm, as I did not feel her idea was very helpful.

"Seriously, you want us to go to the bar across the street and mention we are dropping off a carload of stuff, including a TV, coffee maker, pillows, and bedding for a formerly homeless guy who's now your neighbor. Welcome to the neighborhood! I am sure they'll be thrilled to allow us to unload the truck. Sure, you can unload those treasures right there next to the jukebox in the bar."

I could just hear them saying, "Yes, please, pull the U-Haul around; I'll get the boys to help you unload."

No, thanks for the suggestion Christy but this one isn't going to fly.

Her other suggestion, to ask a neighbor to hold it for him, was equally comical. This area isn't *Straight Outta Compton*, but it certainly isn't suburbia. And if Mike hasn't yet met his neighbors, I didn't plan to either! As we sat in the car we got very silly. Jokes began to circle based upon his name. "Mike" became "Marc

Anthony" and Gigi and I became the J Lo's. In heavily accented Italian, we took turns calling for "Marc Anthony," wondering loudly where he was.

"Marc Anthony, it's the J Lo's. We have your stuff!"

"Marc Anthony, where are you... don't you know it's the J Lo's?"

"Marc Anthony... over here!"

After what seemed like an eternity of laughing and once our cheeks were sufficiently sore from the giggles, we decided we would wait no longer. We would leave the items. It was obvious our sanity depended upon it!

Both Tammy and Gigi's husband were tired of the goods being stored in their garages and would not be happy to see them return. We said a silent prayer that the items would not be stolen, but then decided it didn't really matter if they were; they were likely still going to someone in need. You can rationalize anything if you really want to, and we were at that point.

We told the roofers next door we were leaving the items for Mike. If they had designs on stealing it, they would at least know we suspected them. And then we wrote a note that showed we were kind of losing it. Or maybe it proved we had already lost it.

We wanted to leave a note on the front door for Mike saying that we left his Welcome Wagon at the back door. But as we considered this further, it probably wasn't the best idea to advertise to the neighbors that not only was Mike not there, but we had left all of his belongings at the back door.

"Hey neighbors, we've got a whole bunch of new stuff sitting on the back porch, please come and steal from me."

There were a number of versions of this Post-it note as we cracked ourselves up coming up with alternative text.

"Marc Anthony, the J Lo's were here and you weren't. We left your loot at the back door."

We made light of our frustration as time ticked away, not able to get back to the many things waiting for us at home.

We eventually settled on something more innocuous and less threatening than "check your back door," which sounded like we were leaving a bomb. We tucked the note under the screen door, hoped for the best, and went home, where we could resume discussions about "The Crazy Cleansers" and the joys of juice. By the way, in case you are wondering, I do not recommend any of the cleansing routines proposed by Tammy and Gigi. They seem to all involve massive amounts of bathroom time and additional cleaning. Enough said.

Finally making it back home in one piece, we hugged goodbye and thanked God for protecting us while doing His work, which has become a pretty regular prayer for us since our outing to Braddock and beyond. We later found out that Mike did get the items we had left.

Without much time for a break, a new Welcome Wagon was hastily arranged for the following week. I think the three of us just really wanted to hang out again, and this was as good an excuse as any. What's a little danger in exchange for an afternoon of laughter with friends? We really needed to decompress as many sad things were happening simultaneously.

Another one of our past Welcome Wagon recipients was close to being evicted because he was behind on rent. He had secured Section 8 housing for the future, but it would not take effect for another couple weeks. During the gap in coverage he would likely be back on the streets. We were scrambling to figure out a way to not lose all the stuff that had been donated, but also not to set a precedent of moving people multiple times and getting too involved.

And then there was another man and his baby we were all pretty upset about. Jake was a regular to the Sunday meal, along with his girlfriend. She was completely disinterested in those of us who served, wearing earphones and only removing them for a cursory introduction. Jake's girlfriend wasn't truly homeless, but often joined Jake at our meals. She was a couch surfer, moving from place to place. Here's the unfortunate part: not only was this couple largely living on the street, they were also expecting a child. Weeks later, Jake's girlfriend went into labor and delivered a beautiful baby boy.

Unfortunately, Jake never got to see the baby as he was arrested upon arrival at the hospital. He had an outstanding warrant for his arrest (we never heard for what) and was arrested in the waiting room. It was a truly sad story and such a rough start in life for the baby, who our hearts went out to. Mom bounced from home to home after being released from the hospital.

Previously, Christy had thrown a baby shower for a homeless mom and the entire MFM community had pitched in. Helping this mom and her child was one of those "this is why we do this moments."

This time, we wanted to help mom and baby, but didn't have much of a relationship with her. While Jake was in jail, mom ended up meeting another man and moved in with him. The man she moved in with may have abused the baby, who ended up in the hospital. While the details of what happened were sketchy, we were distraught.

It makes me sick to think about this poor innocent baby who entered the world under such a terrible start. Eventually, the baby found a new home in the foster care system. With Jake still in jail, there was little he could do.

It was quite the mess and these circumstances had really been weighing heavily on our hearts.

But in the midst of it all, we drove to see Dino a week after Mike's Welcome Wagon.

Dino was a veteran who had been living in the Mon Wharf area during his stay on the street. He had been outside for eight months and had formed some close friendships with a few guys also living outdoors. They were all employed at downtown restaurants (upscale restaurants), and apparently, they were close to getting into housing as well.

Dino greeted us warmly at the door. His long, greasy hair was pulled into some semblance of a messy ponytail. His clothes looked clean, although oversized. He lit up when he saw that Gigi had secured a very warm Steeler's jacket for him. Score! Remember, home team apparel is a huge hit for the homeless, regardless if you're a fan or not.

Dino's Welcome Wagon was different than any of the others I participated in, mostly because of the area he was living in. It was actually pretty nice - a lot of row houses and street parking, but it felt much safer than the other locations we had frequented in the past. Dino was different too. He was polite to excess, and kept calling us "ma'am" and thanking us. He was overjoyed with what we brought for him. We unloaded on the curb after a quick greeting, and he said he would carry the belongings inside himself. Most likely, he didn't want us to see how he lived, but he told us it was because it was two flights of stairs up. We respected his wishes and offered to wait with the items on the street to prevent theft, something now important to us.

Standing outside on the sidewalk, Dino told us about his friends; friends who were trying to get out from under the bridge. He said he was going to let the three of them crash with him for awhile to help them get back on their feet. They all worked together at the restaurant, but Dino was the first to secure housing. We again witnessed the generosity of the homeless, offering what little they had to others in need.

We said our goodbyes and went back on our way.

We smiled and thanked each other in the car for doing something good for a guy that wanted to make good. We also remarked about the insanity of the "system."

Before we met Dino, he had completed drug rehab in Erie, PA and was released in May to a shelter in Pittsburgh (over two hours away). How difficult it must have been to be moved to an unfamiliar city with no friends or support system after completing such a grueling treatment. After a very short stay, Dino decided shelter living wasn't for him and he instead chose to live on the street.

I pictured trying to stay clean after struggling with addiction while living outside. I decided it likely wouldn't happen and I felt a great respect for Dino's strength and inner fortitude. Dino would now have shampoo and soap, among other items, courtesy of people he would never know. We left hoping he would clean himself up and get on with his life, putting this dark chapter behind him.

Chapter 16

WHO CALLED THE POLICE?

"We are fiercely Loved by God so we can fiercely Love other people."

Margaret Feinberg

Over 18 months had passed, and the various ministries associated with our original group were still going. Natalie's Bible Project had a full team of people devoted to its world-wide success and sharing of the Word. It has thousands of followers on Facebook, and many Bibles have been decorated in less than two short years since we began this journey. The Bible ministry had expanded, and now Bibles were also going to people fighting cancer or illness, those experiencing a hard time, and really anyone in physical or spiritual need.

I personally received a Bible from Natalie, lovingly decorated, and I gave out a few as well.

The Welcome Wagon has continued and has become its own full-fledged ministry. At last count, our team had provided a full housewarming to 30 people. In addition, a volunteer through Mission from Mars had also been providing Welcome Wagons, adding another 17 people to the list of people who were loved by this compassionate group of people.

But all was not well. With the growth of the Sunday lunch, we were starting to see some trouble. When you get over 100 homeless people together on the street, they are often tired and freezing cold or exceedingly hot. They're always hungry. Things can go wrong. Fights can happen whether verbally or physically. Threats can be made. Items can be stolen or fought over. Food can run out, or maybe there isn't enough for multiple helpings. Small things can turn into big ones and this is simply a reality of life on the streets. Add in the fact that some of the people coming to lunch are abusing alcohol or drugs, and you can easily see how dangerous circumstances could arise.

With the growth in the number of volunteers, there were growing pains as well. While things seemed to be in check at the lunches for the most part, there was growing discontent. With new groups of volunteers coming and going, they weren't as invested in getting to know the homeless. To make room for new volunteers, many of the core team stepped away to allow new people to take ownership of the day and feel a sense of purpose. However, losing that personal connection between the hungry and the servers introduced more challenges. The feeling of fellowship began to erode, and when our early team did go back, it felt different. It was different because we were no longer directly connected to preparing the food, organizing the volunteers, and befriending those coming for lunch. In growing the ministry and involving even more of the community (and way more homeless), things had changed.

How do we keep the community feel at the lunch? The volunteers serving were connecting with one another and the developing compassion was evident. But without that bond with the homeless, things were starting to subtly break down. It was summer, and being hot and homeless isn't quite as bad as being freezing cold, but it can be pretty close.

Without access to air conditioning, it can be impossible to cool off. Lacking access to sunscreens and lip balms, skin can easily dry out and get burned. Thirst and dehydration can become big issues, and the teams serving the meals were seeing this firsthand. Volunteers were providing ice and cold drinks, but ice melts quickly and isn't easy to keep frozen without refrigeration. Even coolers that had been donated to the camps were unable to keep food fresh for long.

It was under this backdrop of brewing unrest that our small team made our next Welcome Wagon, and it brought up some new questions.

How far am I willing to go?

What am I willing to risk to help someone else?

Most of us rarely have a need to ask ourselves these questions, especially when we exist in our safe, comfortable surroundings.

We had been delivering cheer and "making people's days," as Christy would say. While we encountered some bad neighborhoods and shady parts of town, for the most part, our experiences had been "positive." Of course, we had some adventures along the way.

The "positive" part is mostly true. We did have a "funny" experience where Tammy and Gigi accidentally interrupted a drug deal on the side of the road, announcing themselves in proud fashion as the Welcome Wagon. I wish I could have Gigi and Tammy retell it for you, the highly amusing way they go back and forth between them as they recall the details. The story goes something like this:

Tammy: "We rolled up in the minivan, with Booty in the backseat, to the North Side. There was a group of people sitting around doing nothing. I said, "I have a delivery" and everyone scattered."

Gigi: "Actually, it started with Tammy leaning out the window of the minivan with a HUGE smile and saying, 'Are you waiting for a DELIVERY?' The girls got up and booked it out of there."

As I understand the rest of the story, there were some assurances by Tammy and Gigi to the remaining men that they weren't cops - and they blessed the drug dealers with the sign of the cross. After telling them they were from a church, they were left alone. I can almost hear them saying, "No, no, it's ok guys; we're just here doing God's work" or some other variation to get some sympathy, protection, and maybe a little divine intervention.

Eventually they found the intended recipient, who was waiting from a distance at the next corner watching them intently, and I believe, praying for their safety. We were told more than once by our homeless friends that we had more guts than brains, and I suspect interrupting drug deals is a no-no on the street.

There was another incident when we got stuck on the side of the road in Tammy's minivan and the rear sliding door would literally not close. The hysterics involved with four women, and of course Booty, trying to get the door to close was something that could have easily been in a movie.

"Just try pulling on it." One of us would say, as if she hadn't considered that option.

"Yeah. Why didn't I think of that!" Tammy would say back, but in sweet Tammy fashion there wasn't a hint of sarcasm.

We considered driving back with the door open, but since it was Booty's seat, we were pretty worried he might fall out. The recipient of the Welcome Wagon items, and even a repairman working on a house next door, got in on the action - pushing, pulling, tugging, and eventually disassembling fuses and other components we thought could be causing the problem.

Spoiler Alert: None of these parts were the problem.

Did I mention none of us are particularly mechanically inclined?

In a better neighborhood, we probably would have called AAA and waited, but given our location there was a sense of urgency. We would get the door closed. After nothing worked, Tammy decided to drive around the block, and miraculously, when she hit a flat spot in the road, the door was able to close. It was a good thing too, as all of our calls to hubbies were unanswered. Actually, that's not entirely true. My husband answered, but at the time was driving a tiny two door FIAT, and it was quickly realized he would be of no use in rescuing the five of us.

So yeah, we had had some adventures. But nothing like what we were about to encounter.

It was now August of 2017. Tammy and Gigi needed some back-up, or maybe just a laugh, and asked me to join them to deliver for two more friends who secured housing. I'd delivered to this area once before, although I didn't realize it until we were literally across the street from the prior location. The first visit, for the winner of the "Frostbite Lottery," went off without a hitch. As always, I prayed for the same.

I didn't know the person we were blessing. His name was Ryan, and he was newly off the street and in a transitional housing program. We pulled the SUV up to the location and got ready to unload. We tried calling Ryan, but when he didn't pick up, we were forced to go to the door. I pushed the doorbell-style call button to no avail. My partner in delivery, Gigi, stayed in the car with my daughter, who was home from school that day. Tammy had to cancel, so it was just the 2.5 of us.

I began to get the fight or flight feeling of nerves in my stomach, stronger than I had felt in prior experiences, which signaled sure trouble for me. As time had gone on, these nerves were not as easily activated, so I knew something was amiss. A few yards away, and moving closer with every step, two men were screaming profanities at one another. I quickly turned towards another man, who had obviously been drinking and smelled heavily of alcohol. Most of his teeth were missing, the remaining ones covered in strange, sticky-looking pinks and greens.

"Can you tell me how to get inside?" I asked quickly.

The toothless man seemed nice enough, and he immediately pulled out his keys. Even drunk or high, he seemed to have an awareness that I should not be standing outside on the street. The door swung open, and in I went. The pins and needles were more pronounced now as I entered the stark institutional "home" of our friend. Thankfully, a woman appeared to see what I was doing and had been ready for our arrival. We stepped into a room next to the door to call down for Ryan, but before she could the ruckus outside followed us indoors.

There had been two men fighting in front of the door before I went inside. One was big, tall, and quite scary; the other I barely glimpsed. The big man entered the building, and the woman who worked there seemed concerned. It seemed he had gotten past their safety door. He obviously didn't belong.

The big man was now screaming about a white woman who knew his name and was harassing him.

Could he be talking about me? I wondered from the room just feet away?

I hadn't spoken to the man and had no idea what kind of slight I could have imposed.

Could he have been talking about Gigi? Did she get out of the car? Many scenarios were running through my head trying to figure out if we were somehow involved. Most of them ended up with the thought that this guy was dangerous, and I needed to get out of there, quickly.

Waiting in a large, open room just next to the belligerent man, I felt like a sitting duck. Deftly, I excused myself telling the woman as I passed that I would wait in the car. I navigated the gauntlet that was the man in front of me, hoping that my removal from the situation would de-escalate it. Passing just a few inches from the man, I quickly skirted out the door.

When I arrived on the sidewalk, I was greeted by Gigi, who was standing outside the car. She had heard the man screaming about a white woman harassing him and came out of the car in solidarity. Just as the profanity-spewing man made his way through the door after us, I quickly prodded her to get in the car. I feared for us and particularly for my daughter, who was sitting in the rear of the SUV. I was grateful for the car's tinted windows and was hopeful that she hadn't been seen.

As we retreated to the car, we watched in horror as the big man began punching another man randomly. I am not sure if this was the second man from the shouting match that was happening when we arrived, but it did not appear to be provoked. The victim had been talking on his phone on the sidewalk just outside the door. Without any warning, the big man began pummeling Cell Phone Guy's stomach without mercy. In a completely bizarre twist, Cell Phone Guy did not resist. Instead, he calmly set down his phone and took off his shirt (I have no idea why!).

If this wasn't bizarre enough, the deranged man then grabbed Cell Phone Guy and put him into a choke hold, squeezing the breath out of him while we pulled away from the curb.

We were all watching so intently and couldn't figure out what to do. Do we try to help Cell Phone Guy? But how? Both men were much bigger, tougher, and stronger than we were, and we had Alexa in the back seat. We were beyond terrified, especially considering he might have thought we were in some way involved.

I'd like to say we were brave and stopped the fight, but we didn't. We quickly surmised that the next action was going to involve something worse, like a gun, and we were petrified. We swerved right onto the next street, trying to catch our breath and calm our nerves. There really wasn't another way out without turning the car around, and we wanted to see what was happening from a safe distance away.

As we rounded the corner, four police cars arrived and split up the men. From our vantage point in the car, we could see both of the men being cuffed on the hoods of police cruisers. A large crowd surrounded the brawlers and police in the street, which was fascinating to me given the time of day, it wasn't yet lunch time. I was again reminded of the additional dangers when there are large groups of men outside during the day, with seemingly nothing to do.

Street Fight. Photo taken after police arrived

We continued to watch and wait from a half a block away.

While we sat there collecting ourselves and calming our nerves, we called Christy to explain the situation. She encouraged us to go back to the location (given the police presence), but we were still very unsure.

We were conflicted about fulfilling this delivery. On one hand, the car was filled and we didn't really want to unload it back at Gigi's. The prospect of coming back again was equally unpleasant. But, on the other hand, we felt like we had just risked our lives for some housewares and weren't keen on the idea of doing so again today.

After much consideration, we decided we would drive back up to the curb and see what the situation looked like. If it looked safe, we would try to make the delivery. If we had a bad feeling, we would quickly depart.

It seemed meant to be when we arrived on the corner and found the woman from the shelter talking to another. We rolled down the windows and excitedly asked her what had just happened. She explained that the dangerous looking, big man was trying to get into their building and the Cell Phone Guy wouldn't let him in. They seemed to think the comments about the white woman were about someone else, so at least we had that going for us.

While it didn't appear this kind of thing happened every day, it certainly didn't seem to be as unusual as we found it. We were grateful for the quick thinking of the shelter employee that likely saved Cell Phone Guy's life by calling the police. We were told that both men were drunk and had been arrested. I wondered if there was more than alcohol involved.

As we continued to talk to the shelter employee and a woman on the street, I wish I could say that the situation became more normal - that we could simply deliver our goods; but, of course, it didn't.

While the danger had passed, there was a woman on the other side of the road talking, yelling, ranting, and singing to herself, I think all at the same time.

One of the women we were talking to remarked, "That lady's crazy yo. She out there all da time. Just crazy."

We asked the shelter worker if we could drop the items off with her since we had been having trouble reaching our intended recipient. It was then that she told us that Ryan was a really nice guy, almost entirely deaf, which was probably why he wasn't answering the phone. Guilt began to pile up, as we had been silently cursing him for not picking up his phone during repeated attempts. We realized how difficult it must be for him. I couldn't fathom being homeless and deaf, lacking one of the key senses that could help protect oneself on the street. I was so glad he was now indoors, and we happily unloaded the SUV onto the sidewalk.

We didn't wait to ensure everything was inside; we were ready to move on. The worker assured us that she would take care of it, and we trusted her. We also figured, as we did at the prior Etna delivery, that if any of the people nearby took it, they were almost all certainly in need.

We finally left and had a dejected feeling that we still had one more delivery to make. We really weren't excited about it at that point, having reached our limit of near death experiences for one day.

In the car, we reflected on what we were doing and who we were doing it for. We were seeing Jesus in the people we were blessing, but began to wonder if we were going about it the right way.

With the Welcome Wagon, we encountered potential risk to ourselves and even our loved ones. We didn't know Ryan. We risked a bad neighborhood and possible harm to give him a few simple household items.

It made us question to one another, "Was it worth it?"

"Would it be worth it if something happened to us or one of our children?"

Later in the week, as a group, we wrestled with these questions. In the last couple of Welcome Wagons we described, we were helping random strangers, people that Christy had simply referred to us.

"Are we making the right decisions?"

The Welcome Wagon began as an outpouring of love for our friends, people we knew and trusted to some degree.

"Are we really helping; and if so, at what potential cost?"

We didn't find the answer that day in the return car ride, nor have we found it since. We did, however, deliver a second Welcome Wagon in Etna, just a couple doors down from "Marc Anthony," whose delivery had made us laugh so much. Our smiles returned in the safer confines. We teased each other about who should go into the bar to ask if they will hold our items until our recipient came home. As it turned out, no bar assistance was required. Our guy was waiting eagerly for us outside his home.

He was excited for what we brought him, sharing briefly his struggles. He was in obvious need and was quite grateful, and we left feeling fulfilled and even a bit at peace.

The homeless are complicated. Questions arose for our group that we never would have previously considered. There are ethical dilemmas and even spiritual ones, and they are both tough to wrestle with. I would love to say that I could provide advice given my personal experience, but even now, two years after beginning this journey, I don't feel competent to do so. I want people to lead with their heart, but also to be careful. Maybe if we had more than switchblade combs and pepper spray we would have felt more comfortable, but I doubt it. Undoubtedly, there are many people in law enforcement who might want to avoid areas we have been to, under bridges, in alleyways, and even some of our delivery areas.

Which brings me back to where this story begins, with the convicted sex offender the police were searching for who had eaten with us regularly. I am reminded of him because of another tragic story in the news, a story about a man on the run who had been hiding from the police. The headline in the article in the online Tribune Review newspaper read, **"Suspect in Ohio toddler's rape and murder hitchhiked, lived in woods for weeks before arrest."** The news account follows below:

MARY ANN THOMAS | _Friday, Oct. 27, 2017, 5:12 a.m._

PittsburghTribuneReview.com

"A man accused of raping and murdering a 13-month-old girl in Ohio hitched a ride to Western Pennsylvania and spent weeks living in the woods before Franklin Park police arrested him early Friday, authorities said.

"We shrunk his world and he had no choice but to live in the woods," said Pete Elliott, U.S. Marshal for the Northern District of Ohio.

Joshua Gurto, 37, is charged with rape and aggravated murder in the Oct. 7 death of Sereniti Jazzlynn-Sky Blankenship-Sutley in Conneaut, Ohio, a small town in the northeastern corner of the state.

... Shortly before 2 a.m. Friday, Franklin Park patrolman Kevin Lestitian saw a man with a large backpack walking along the borough's Nicholson Road, near Wexford Bayne Road. The location is about 5 miles north of the Sheetz store in Ohio Township and about 5 miles south of the Pennsylvania Turnpike.

"It's a state road with no sidewalks. Anyone walking along that road at 1:30 or so in the morning is going to attract attention. Any officer seeing that would stop and ask the person if they are OK," Franklin Park Sgt. Walter Healy said.

Lestitian identified Gurto and took him into custody without incident.

The patrolman found a number of items in Gurto's backpack, including maps of Pennsylvania and New Jersey and a tent. Gurto also had a knife in his possession, Elliott said.

Gurto is in Allegheny County Jail awaiting extradition."

This man, this homeless man who was living in the woods, could have been one of our Sunday lunch guests. He was found a short distance away from our food service, and if he was trying to avoid being spotted he likely avoided the larger shelters. The idea hit me again that it was possible that our efforts had gone to this man. Maybe we doled out a special second helping of food for him. Maybe someone made him a special meal. Maybe someone from our group, or Mission from Mars, had given him the tent they had found with him. All of these maybes intensified my feelings of guilt and frustration.

So today, I struggle with what we are doing. We've offered food and clothing, but more than that too. We've provided welcome and love in this community that has been developing over a two year period - this safe place where homeless and non-homeless have joined together to eat and talk and laugh.

People who came to eat with us found food and fellowship. They found information and referrals to help in terms of shelters and places to go. And for the repeats, especially the people we met in early 2016, they found friendship and community.

Could a few bad apples really spoil the bunch?

Chapter 17

AND THIS IS HOW IT ENDS

"Your voice has the power to transform individuals and communities: your family, your friends, the multitude, and the one person on your doorstep. And if you will just risk starting with a whisper, oh, what could happen."

Office for Lay Collaboration in Ministry
Archdiocese of Bombay

I learned a lot over the past two years as I have been writing this book. I have been privileged to meet some of the most inspiring people and have more laughs than anyone should have while dealing with desperate circumstances. The bonds we forged with those who served together, or with people we never would have met, talked to, or even perhaps looked at, have changed us. We have become different people for having this experience, more compassionate and willing to see the good in others, even when we can also see the bad. We have shown love and have been shown love and sincere gratitude.

We have given people the tools to change lives if they decide to do so, but have also found that we can't change people. In our encounters, we had people take advantage of our generosity. They lied to us and conned us for their own purposes. They sold things we gave them, like sleeping bags they had begged for or tents they swore they needed. They pushed and tested our patience and our resolve. They made us question whether or not we should help the homeless at all, whether they were a lost cause. But at the end of the day when I look back, all I can see is the change the experience has made in the people who volunteered.

I see the way my children look with compassion and mercy at people who they never would have looked at or seen before. I see my daughter purchasing ham at a deli in the Strip District of Pittsburgh because she saw a homeless man on the street in obvious need of food.

I see my husband having an unsolicited conversation with people on the street, showing a form of compassion I never knew he had. I see the relationships that have developed with people like Tammy, Gigi, and Natalie, people I either wouldn't have known, or would have never known this deeply. And I see the transformation that has happened within Christy, who when we first met was still healing from her own deep wounds and is now running a group that has helped so many and from which so much good has come.

And, when I look back now at the person I was before all of this came into my life, I see a change in myself. I am at peace. I have received an incredible healing of body, as well as mind and spirit, which I attribute to prayer and the anointing I received. In the work we have done, I have found purpose and fulfillment, even if I have also found fear and seen tragedy. It is my hope that someday one of the people we met will recall a single smile, a kind word, or item that we gave them. It's my hope that in knowing that someone cared, it changed their life too.

For me, it was worth it for that one person, whether homeless or suburban neighbor.

This is how it ends?

I always thought the end of the story would involve one of us dying. Yes, that sounds terrible to say, but the situations we were putting ourselves into were dangerous, and we were ill-equipped to handle them. None of us carried a gun or any sort of protection, although we did have our own weapons...our stinky pits if we came straight from the gym, or Gigi's switchblade comb! Regardless, we always felt some sort of divine protection.

What we didn't anticipate was Mission from Mars ending. Sure, it was a long shot at success, a charity that wasn't a charity, but it was so strongly supported by the community that it seemed destined to continue forever. But there was a breaking point.

In November of 2017, Christy informed us that she would be cancelling the Sunday meal service. There had been an incident at the lunch where a screaming match had begun, and the police were called. Thankfully there were no injuries, but the language that was used was inappropriate for the children who witnessed it, and it could have escalated. The school asked Mission from Mars to relocate away from the school, and Christy was at her wit's end. She had also been providing relief efforts related to the hurricanes in Texas, Florida, and Puerto Rico, and she was maxed out.

A couple of our homeless friends had simply vanished, disappeared without a trace leaving us worried and fearful. Others had succumbed to addiction and had overdosed, having to be revived. Another died of an overdose. Some had been arrested and put in jail.

The Be Project group was distraught. I shed a few tears realizing this was the end of an astonishing run, one that could never be replicated. We had done so much and grown so closely together that we didn't want it to end. It was a selfish feeling for us, but it also felt selfish for those on the street - the people who had been relying on Mission from Mars.

The next Sunday, there was no lunch. It was cancelled.

It was as if someone had died. That's how I felt. I felt conflicted and guilty, but I also supported the decision. No one had provided a Welcome Wagon since our last ill-fated adventure, and it seemed like the right decision for now.

"What would we do now? What would they do now?" we questioned aloud with one another.

The proposed Mission from Mars closure did not last long. Christy's inner fortitude was shown as she decided to pick up the pieces and problem solve. Yes, Mission from Mars (like all homeless missions) had some problems, and the past weeks brought them to the forefront. But it had also done so much good for so many, including many of the people who volunteered on its behalf.

When the teams of new volunteers joined in, there was a loss in continuity of volunteers, eroding the feeling of community. To remedy the situation, Christy worked with established ministries crafting a plan to create a safer meal service environment. They decided that the meal would no longer be FOR the homeless, but WITH the homeless, a huge distinction… and one that the Be Project group was thrilled they were making. Mission from Mars supporters began enjoying meals again with friends on the sidewalk and in a park.

Only time will tell what will happen to Mission from Mars and all of our original volunteers from the Be Project, but I am rooting for all of their success. I am rooting for Mission from Mars to continue helping people experiencing homelessness – to help them change their lives and reacclimate into society. I am rooting for our friends on the street to get jobs, start families, and to put their pasts behind them. I am rooting for the volunteers too, the people who think they are going to "help." I am rooting for them to have the types of experience that change their lives, change thinking, and change everything about the way they live. I am rooting for them to have the types of experiences that Christy, Natalie, Gigi and

Tammy have had, that my family has had, and that I, myself, have had.

I have written about my encounters with a lot of remarkable people. Yes, some of them have had struggles, but who among us hasn't? Please know that this book is my recollection of events and perceptions which could be entirely different than someone else's, but I hope that everyone represented in this book knows they are loved by me. All of them are exceptional in their own way, and I am a better person for having known them. Thank you all for helping me become a better version of myself. As I finish this book just a few days before Christmas of 2017, another chapter ends. One of the homeless camps is closed. Crowbar, a man living in the camp, was upset that no one was taking care of a cat that had been frequenting the area. The cat's face had been mangled and was being eaten alive by mites. He was frustrated with the lack of compassion among his brethren and he erupted. A large fight broke out. Authorities arrived to a chaotic scene; heroin use had become rampant at the camp. Vandalism had occurred. The city had reached its limit and sent in a bulldozer.

The camp has been closed permanently. As Christy would say, "So now I got homeless people even more homeless on no notice."

That about sums it up when working with the homeless. There are more problems than solutions, and often they are dire.

It's the end of the story, but also a beginning - a chance for the Christy's of the world to step up, a chance for people to show compassion, and most of all, mercy. We can make meals, we can donate money, and we can give of our time, but to give the gift of mercy is special. It comes from inside your heart, a gift from God. You cannot learn it, just like you cannot learn faith or love. These are gifts freely given to us that our souls desperately need. It is my hope that all who read these words will be inspired and moved to share in these incredible gifts, particularly the gift of mercy.

...AND THIS IS HOW IT ENDS

ACKNOWLEDGMENTS

I couldn't have written this book without the constant love and support of my entire family, including my children and my husband, without whom I never would have served the homeless for the first time. For my parents, in-laws, and extended family for generally influencing the person I am today. For Michelle, Kat, Claire, Leslie, Kelley, and Kim for being people I have relied on for many years, and all of the friends and family I haven't named, who have always encouraged me to pursue my passions.

To the people who have supported my writing, particularly the parishioners and staff.

For my small group and book club from way back, you are all the best. And for our kindergarten mom's group, for giving me sanity years ago when I needed it most.

Robin, Kate, and Dana, I am so grateful for all of your advice and support as first readers and supporters.

For my editors, for their encouragement and passion, particularly Mary, Kirstin, Bob, and Christina, and my fantastic audio and media team, Nick, Rhys, and Mac.

For Sharon, your work with the homeless is inspiring.

Lee and Jen, your cover design work is beautiful.

I would be remiss if I didn't thank the many homeless who became friends and who welcomed me into their lives, as well as the volunteers who participated with John's Meal, Overpass, and the Be Project group, including our neighborhood crew, who have made a difference in so many ways. I hope that you will continue to be advocates and live your talents.

For the shelters and organizations that serve the homeless each day and faithfully execute their missions, without whom many more would be cold and hungry, we all thank you!

Natalie, Christy, Tammy, and Gigi, I am a better person for having met you and can't imagine my life before our crazy escapades, or better people to share the excitement. Keep those combs handy for our next adventures!

For God, who inspires and loves.

AUTHOR'S NOTE: While this is a work of non-fiction, the recollections here are mine alone and may vary from actual events. To provide protection and privacy for the people depicted in this story, I have changed names, locations, and circumstances liberally. Characters depicted are based on composites of people I have known. It was more important for me to protect people's identities rather than create a true and exactly accurate depiction of events.

I apologize for any inaccuracies if they exist. The views contained herein should not be taken to reflect those of any other organization, particularly Mission from Mars, The Bible Project, the Welcome Wagon, any Pittsburgh homeless missions or organizations, or any religion or church.

The views referenced in the book are based upon my early learning and understanding about the homeless. It is possible that over time and with experience, the points of view may change. How a character may answer a question today may differ from how they might have answered it then. As the saying goes, the more we know, the more we know. We have all been learning along the way.

Poverty alleviation is extremely complicated, and this book does not attempt to provide the level of detail and discernment necessary to make fully informed decisions, but failure to understand the breath of poverty should not preclude efforts to help and share our experiences.

Stay in Touch and Post a Review!

jenskyauthor.com

APPENDIX
A Resource Guide to Become More Involved

According to GenerationOn.org, "On average, over 578,000 people are homeless in the U.S. on a given night--31% without shelter." That's over half a million people without a home, bed, or a roof over their head each day. *Homelessness is much more prevalent than most of us know.*

Did you know that in my home state of Pennsylvania, close to half of all people termed "Literally Homeless," have spent **over 1 year** living outdoors or in short term homeless shelters?

There are things that you can do and resources that are available to help.

What can I do as an individual?

Learn More. By learning more about the plights of friends and neighbors, we become more compassionate.

Consider volunteering your time at a local homeless shelter or other organization that provides for the material, spiritual, and emotional needs of the homeless. Who knows, you might make a new friend!

Prayer. The number one request I have received from the homeless is for my prayers.

In talking about the homeless, it's easy to feel intimidated. So, I urge you to do one small thing…when you pass a homeless person on the street, don't cross the street. Simply look at them directly and make eye contact. You can say hello or ask them to join you for a cup of coffee. Or, you could even start-up a conversation, asking where they are from, or what sports teams they cheer on. If all else fails, most everyone likes to talk about the weather!

You may just find that in meeting someone new and seeing them as a person, that you might become inspired to do more. If you aren't yet feeling direct interaction, that's ok too. We are all uniquely gifted. Maybe you are being called to be behind the scenes in some other way. Not everyone is needed to do the same things, but…we are all called to love our neighbor.

What can my Church, Neighborhood Group, Scouts, or Student Group do?

Consider hosting a drive to collect items that might be needed for the homeless in your area based upon the time of year. In the summer, lip balm and sunscreen are appreciated; in the winter, coats, hats, gloves, and hand warmers are sought after items. You can collect from friends and neighbors, or at school, church, or local businesses. These items can be given out personally on the streets, or through a local organization. I encourage you to consider your donations carefully, ensuring they are clean and usable. For many on the street, doing laundry is a luxury.

You could also gather together with friends to make a meal. At our church we created a Meal Making Ministry, inspired by our "John's Meal" cooking experience. This ministry has now grown significantly, and at our last event, we made food for over 1000 people and had 100 volunteers participate. It's a great way to involve kids too! They can prepare food, package blessing bags, and they love to make special cards and other items to show they care. You can share these blessings with local organizations in need.

Be aware that different areas of the country have different rules related to the homeless and some cities even have bans on food sharing in public places. Make sure to learn about your local area by talking with local law enforcement or shelter staff.

Want to Read More?

Yankoski, Michael. *Under the Overpass: a Journey of Faith on the Streets of America.* Multnomah Books, 2010. Firsthand account of living among the homeless on the streets of several major cities.

Corbett, Steve et al. *When Helping Hurts, How to Alleviate Poverty Without Hurting the Poor… and Yourself.* Moody Publishers, 2014. A discussion of poverty alleviation and how to help without hurting those in need.

Gunning, Monica et al. *A Shelter in Our Car.* Children's Book Publishing, 2014. Introduction to homelessness through the eyes of a child.

Lupton, Robert. *Toxic Charity: how churches and charities hurt those they help (and how to reverse it).* HarperOne, 2012. Details the "toxic" effects of some charities efforts to help.

Government and Other Resources

HUD Exchange connects those who are homeless or at risk of becoming homeless with nearby resources - *Hudexchange.info*

National Health Care for Homeless Council - *nhchc.org*

National Coalition for the Homeless - *Nationalhomeless.org*

US Department of Health and Human Services, Resources for Persons Experiencing Homelessness - *HHS.gov*

National Runaway safe line is there to listen whether you are thinking of running away or already have - *1800runaway.org*

Substance Abuse and Mental Health Services Administration - *Samhsa.gov*

REFLECTION QUESTIONS

1. What did you like most about this book?
2. If you were making a movie about this book, who would you cast? What scene best lends itself to the big screen?
3. When you think about the homeless as people rather than problems, what does this mean to you? Do you agree?
4. Share a favorite quote from the book, why did it stand out?
5. If you knew you were providing a tarp or food to someone who was wanted by the police, would you still do it? Would knowledge of what their crime was impact your decision whether or not to offer aid (theft versus murder)?
6. What feelings and emotions did this book evoke for you? How does your lens impact how you felt while reading?
7. Did anything in the book make you feel inspired to act? If not, what is holding you back?
8. Did Jen, Natalie, and Christy seem like regular people like you, or did they seem to possess more gifts, talents, or faith than others? What about Evander, Yvonne, and Major?
9. When John didn't come for the meal that was made especially for him, the group questioned why. How

would you have felt if you were Natalie? What if you were John?

10. When Jen encountered the broken man with the frozen beard, she felt an incredible sadness. What would you have done differently in that situation?

11. Jen lamented that the shelters were not open during the day. Do you think this should be changed? If so, how? What are the barriers to this happening?

12. Natalie believed that John's meal was just half of what was needed, the other half being the Bibles she distributed. Was one more necessary than the other?

13. Having faith is not required to do good works – an atheist can serve the homeless and be charitable. What role does faith play in the story? What role does faith play in serving others?

14. Many of the people in the book brought their children with them to serve. What benefits do you see for the children and the homeless? What are the drawbacks or concerns?

15. Which character in the book impacted you most? Were they a homeless person or someone who went to serve? Why did you choose this person? What part of their story resonated most with you?

16. If you could have lunch with one person in the book and hear the rest of their story, who would it be and why?

17. If you could ask the author one question, what would it be?

18. What did you think of the book's title and cover? How did they relate to the story?

CPSIA information can be obtained
at www.ICGtesting.com
Printed in the USA
LVHW101339160420
653663LV00020B/3401